You Belong In Tech

How To Go From Zero Programming Knowledge To Hired

By Anna Jean McDougall

ANNA JEAN MCDOUGALL

Copyright © 2022 Anna Jean McDougall
All rights reserved.

Table of Contents

INTRODUCTION 7

SECTION 1 WHAT YOU NEED DEVELOPING YOUR TECHNICAL SKILLS 15

   CHAPTER 1 LEARNING MENTALITY 18
      Recognition vs Recall 18
      The Dunning-Kruger Effect 20
      Imposter Syndrome 21

   CHAPTER 2 WHAT SKILLS, TOOLS, OR PROGRAMMING LANGUAGES SHOULD YOU LEARN? 25
      Essential Skill #1: A Programming Language 26
      Essential Skill #2: An Integrated Developer Environment (IDE) or 'Code Editor' 27
      Essential Skill #3: Basic Command Line 29
      Essential Skill #4: Version Control 30
      Essential Skill #5: Searching the Internet 33

   CHAPTER 3 HOW CAN I LEARN PROGRAMMING GIVEN MY LIFE CIRCUMSTANCES? 36
      Options for Learning Programming in Person (*at least traditionally!) 37
      Options for Self-Learning Online 49
      What is 'Documentation' and How Do I Use It? 64

   CHAPTER 4 CREATING A LEARNING PLAN USING AGILE METHODOLOGIES 68
      Introduction to Scrum 69
      Using Scrum as a Framework For a Learning Plan 71
      Final Remarks on My 'Agile Learning' Approach 78

   CHAPTER 5 NON-PROGRAMMING JOBS 80
      Product Owner 81
      Scrum Masters and Project Managers 82
      UI/UX Designers 84
      Tech Recruiters 85

Developer Advocates 86
KEY TAKEAWAYS 88

SECTION 2 WHO YOU ARE   FINDING YOUR IDENTITY AND GROWING A COMMUNITY 90

CHAPTER 6 CREATING A BRAND IDENTITY AND USING THE TRICKS OF THE TRADE 94
Branding and the Three-Words Approach 96
Unique Selling Point 99
The Elevator Pitch 101

CHAPTER 7 SOCIAL MEDIA PROFILES: DOS AND DON'TS 104
Cover Image 105
Profile Picture 107
Short Description or Byline 108
Long Description/About Me 111
Pinned Posts 111

CHAPTER 8 TYPES OF COMMUNITIES AND EVENTS 113

CHAPTER 9 THE (MOSTLY) UNWRITTEN RULES OF CODING COMMUNITIES 117
Read Their Rules And Guidelines 117
Don't Ask To Ask 118
Provide Code Examples 118
Outline What You've Already Tried 119
Be Honest When You Don't Understand 120
Accept Criticism Gracefully 120
Bonus Tip: The Rubber Duck Technique 121

CHAPTER 10 MENTORING AND COACHING 123
Mentorship vs Coaching 124
So When Should I Get a Mentor and How Do I Find One? 125
How to Benefit from a Mentor 126

CHAPTER 11 THE SPECIAL ROLE OF BLOGGING IN SOFTWARE DEVELOPMENT 128
What Should I Write About? I'm Just a Beginner! 129
Blog Hosting: Things to Consider 132
Structuring and Writing a Blog Post 133
English as a Second Language 136

CHAPTER 12 BECOMING A SOCIAL MEDIA HIT: BUILDING A COMMUNITY BY GOING BEYOND THE SURFACE 138

Tip 1: Keep the Audience in Mind 140
Tip 2: Stop the Scroll, Use a Hook 142
Tip 3: Engage with Big Accounts 145
Tip 4: Use Relevant Hashtags and Keywords 146
Tip 5: Use Private Messaging 147

KEY TAKEAWAYS 150

SECTION 3 HOW YOU GET THERE APPLYING AND INTERVIEWING FOR JOBS 153

CHAPTER 13 'HOW DO I KNOW I'M READY?' MENTAL PREPARATION FOR THE JOB SEARCH 156
Just Apply 157
Technical Milestones 158
Lean on Contacts or a Mentor 160
Reach Out to Recruiters 161
Freelance to Fill the Gap 162

CHAPTER 14 WHAT JOBS ARE AVAILABLE? WHERE SHOULD I LOOK? 164
Startups 165
Small To Medium Tech Companies 166
Big Tech Companies 167
Agencies/Consultancies 168
Normal Companies With Tech Departments 170

CHAPTER 15: CREATING AN APPLICATION KIT 172
How Much or How Little to Mention Your Former Career 174
CVs, Resumes, and Work History Profiles 176
Visually Stunning vs Basic Text CVs 176
Make Contact Easy 178
Structuring CVs with No Technical Work History 178
A Short Note on Skills 180
Describe Achievements, Not Duties 180
Portfolio and Projects 181
Cover Letters 184
Using LinkedIn Effectively 187

CHAPTER 16 APPLYING TO JOBS 189
Collection of Information 192
Adaptation of Documents 194
Recruiter Contact 198
Application 200

CHAPTER 17 UNDERSTANDING THE CLASSIC JOB INTERVIEW STAGES FOR TECH 201
    Screening Call 202
    First Interview (Mostly Social) 204
    Second Interview (Technical) 205
    Other Types Of Interviews That Can Occur 208

CHAPTER 18 INTERVIEW PREPARATION 210
    Technical Preparation 211
    Physical and Mental Preparation 214
    On-Site Interviews 215
    Video Interviews 217
    Practising Common Interview Questions 219

CHAPTER 19 AFTER THE INTERVIEW 224
    Should I Send a Follow-Up Message? 225
    Dealing with Rejection 226
    The 'One Step Closer' Concept 228
    Lifelong Roommate 228
    Motivation Hits and Becoming Resilient 229
    Taking a Break from the Job Search 230
    Should I Quit Trying to be a Developer? 231
    Final Contact 233
    Dealing with an Offer 233

KEY TAKEAWAYS 236

CONCLUSION 'OH CRAP, I GOT THE JOB. NOW WHAT?' **238**

Introduction

Tech has changed. The pandemic helped change it.

The technology industry is a behemoth, stretching across all other industries and often forming the fundamental building blocks of new products and services. It is increasingly integrated into our everyday lives, from toasters to TVs, from cars to power bills, from music to grocery shopping.

This was, of course, already happening before the events of 2020 hit. Nowadays, we chat to friends on social media, we buy products on online portals, and we book doctor's appointments via app. At a bare minimum, we now expect almost every business we frequent to have a website.

With the advent of COVID, however, these changes accelerated. With lockdowns, it was no longer a matter of wanting online-accessible services, it was a matter of needing online-accessible services. Traditionally in-person activities very quickly required online versions: schools, workplaces, and government agencies all scrambled to put together remote options. Zoom shot into prominence.

This shift in the digital needs of the average citizen will, I'm sure, be rolled back slightly as restrictions continue to be lifted. However, many businesses won't see a full return to in-person work, and many workers will no longer need to live in the same city or state as the company for which they work. This change in the fundamental structure of white-collar work will stretch deep and wide into the need for tech workers.

Luckily for the tech industry, COVID also provided individuals with the opportunity to sit and reflect.

Sometimes, that reflection was borne out of necessity: "I've been fired and nobody is hiring. What do I do now?". Sometimes, that reflection was borne out of increased time at home: "Wow, I have so much more time with my kids. Is there any way I could do this long-term?". Sometimes, that reflection was borne out of an exploration of interests: "I've always wanted to try this. Maybe I should give it a go.". Whatever prompted it, thousands of people were suddenly Googling how to learn programming.

I was one of those people.

When I was 8 years old, I asked my parents to buy me a book about learning HTML at home. I can't for the life of me remember why I wanted this book instead of Animorphs or Goosebumps, but apparently I was quite insistent. This was the mid-90s, when even the best corporate website would be considered a cluttered mess by today's standards. However at this stage, dial-up was still how most people connected to the internet, and CSS (a way to style and design websites) was not yet 'a thing'.

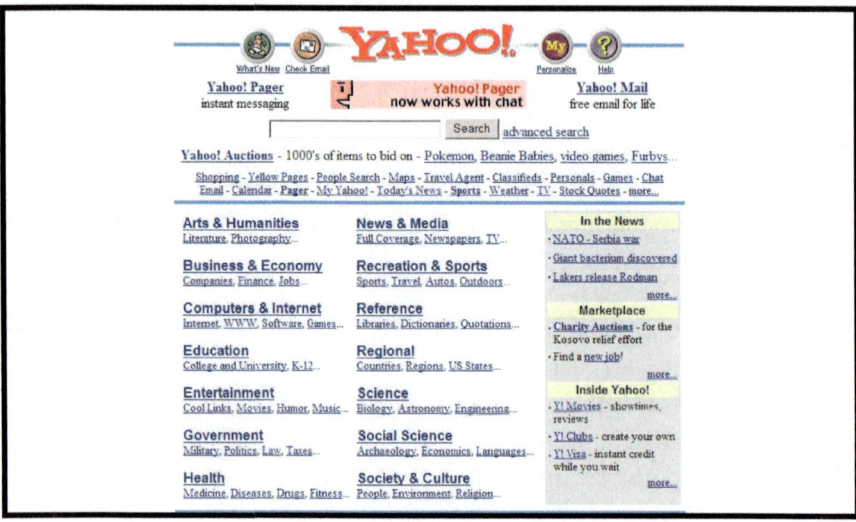

Yahoo! homepage, 1995

My first website was a page of *Father Ted* links, since I used to love watching the BBC comedy with my dad back then. I would scour the internet for good fan pages about the show, then add them to my page. The site even included a "counter", an old-school display of the number of visitors a page got.

A website counter example

When I got to high school, I studied Software Design and Development for one year. It was fine but the topic was new and the teacher inexperienced. I ended up teaching the class about HTML and won a school award thanks to it. However, I was the only girl in the class and despite the well-intentioned boys around me, it was still a socially isolating experience. I had other topics I was good at, in which me being a girl wasn't a "big deal", and in which the teachers knew exactly how to teach their subjects.

By the time I reached university, I had decided to pursue a career in the media. I was good at presenting and writing, and video editing in particular came naturally to me as a great mix of big-picture thinking along with needing a good eye for detail. During the course of my studies, I took every opportunity to choose 'the digital option' for my assignments, including submitting essays in website form.

My communications degree didn't, in the end, lead me into a media career. Rather, I ended up finding a role as a project manager for technical- and safety-based mining conferences. This, in turn, led me into a digital marketing role with Opera Australia. My time there was fundamental in forming my understanding of the digital economy, for example when we hired a software consultancy to build an app for us. However, what ended up drawing me in the most was the music.

After about a year and a half of taking singing lessons with one of the company's singers, using the upstairs practice rooms during my lunch breaks, I auditioned for the Sydney Conservatorium of Music and was accepted into their Masters programme. Thus began my seven-year career as an opera singer, which ended up taking me on tours all around my home state, brought me to Germany to seek full-time work in the Hessen State Theatre, and saw me take up opportunities to sing in Prague and in the USA.

The work was glorious, the people open and friendly, the highs were thrilling and the downs were devastating. I loved the day-to-day work: getting to the theatre, putting on stage makeup, sitting down to have your hair done, singing some of the most fabulous music ever written, doing quick-changes backstage, dancing in ridiculous costumes… It was a thrill!

However, there was still a niggling doubt. Sure, the daily work was great. But I knew there was part of me that wasn't being explored: the part that loved logic and reasoning; the part that was ambitious and driven; the part that wanted to make a tangible difference in the world.

After seven years in the industry and becoming pregnant with my first child, knowing this would mean a move across the country to a new city, I was faced with a dilemma: Do I continue doing this job which I love on a day-to-day level, but which was not satisfying my long-term drives? Or, do I change careers and look for something which can intellectually challenge me and give me opportunities to forge a bigger future?

With the first COVID lockdown in Germany hitting just as my maternity leave ended, and meaning my partner was able to be home and care for our almost-one-year-old, I had the opportunity I needed. We split the day into morning and afternoon 'shifts' with the little one, and mornings were my time to try out coding again.

I was hesitant. After all, by this stage I was a 32-year-old mum with an extremely varied work background, living in a country where I was not totally fluent in the language, and where they value specialising in specific careers from an early age. My image of tech was of young men in their early 20s, none of whom I could picture being super excited about working next to an 'old lady' like me. Was it too late? Would I ever be accepted, even if I did turn out to be good? Would German companies even give me a chance to prove myself?

Luckily for me, I found some terrific online communities which dispelled my fears. Most notably, the Discord community for The Odin Project, and tech Twitter. I had only fleetingly been involved in Twitter before, mostly when I used to stream an online card game called GWENT. This time, I took on the #100DaysofCode challenge and began learning HTML, CSS, and JavaScript. Seeing my progress, people gave me plenty of support. Thanks to the world of Twitter, I also got to see other women developers learning, growing, and working in many different parts of tech: Angie Jones, Emma Bostian, Ali Spittel, and more. Motivational tech tweeters like Danny Thompson kept reassuring me that 32 was, in fact, not at all too old to be making a career change, and I got to hear stories of people in their 50s learning to code. This community lifted me up, gave me confidence, and connected me to wider discussions around programming and technology, allowing me to explore topics I might otherwise have missed, for example around the accessibility of websites for blind and visually impaired people.

It helped that I also loved programming. Something about the way code organised concepts 'clicked' with me, and it was exciting. I had something to contribute here. I had plenty of room to grow, and with technology constantly changing, I would never be bored or become too comfortable. It was exactly what I needed.

I signed up for a one-year web development course with Digital Career Institute (DCI) in Germany; because I was coming out of my maternity leave unemployed, I was eligible for a government sponsorship of my studies. It was supposed to be an in-person course but due to COVID we weren't allowed to meet in person. This meant that I ended up learning web development with about 10 others, entirely online via Zoom.

I quickly grew to realise that the 60 days I had spent self-learning had in fact put me months ahead of my peers. Rather than use the course mainly to learn web development, I used it to better learn how to program in teams. I helped the other students and, as a result, was elected class representative and was also hired by DCI as a class tutor. I was teaching the course while I was learning it: this kept me even more motivated to keep learning and growing my skills so I could stay ahead of the curve.

I found a job before finalising my course. It happened in large part thanks to Twitter, and you'll hear more about it later in the book. However, what all of this taught me is that you do not need structured courses to 'properly' learn the technical skills required to be a good programmer, but the social/networking/teamwork aspect is something where interaction with others is necessary, and that aspect should not be underestimated. Despite its reputation for basement-dwelling super nerds, programming is in most cases a team sport.

This became even more apparent when I was approached after a year of software engineering to become a director of product and engineering for one of Germany's largest media conglomerates. They wanted someone who not only understood the technical side, but who could talk about it on stages around the world, and who could honestly and genuinely relate to people, in order to diversify and create an inclusive environment for engineers of all sorts of backgrounds. Rather than considering only my tech experience, they considered the whole package.

Tech companies around the world are looking for engineers and managers who can both code and communicate.

After my wild ride from marketing to opera to software engineering, I began to get a lot of messages and tweets from others looking to transition into tech. How did I do it? How long would it take them? What programming language should they learn? How do they create a good LinkedIn profile? Why is nobody calling them back when they apply for roles?

The questions were flooding in, and I found I was often repeating myself. So much so, that it was an obvious next step to write a book.

In this book, I use my marketing and project management skills to teach you how to organise your learning and sell your skills to hiring managers; I use my stage skills to teach you how to deal with nerves and how to network with others; and I use my experience as a director of engineering to talk about what the hiring process is like and what technical skills you really need.

Before we begin: let's cover the basics of creating a tech career.

Firstly, there are no hard-and-fast rules when it comes to a career change. For some people, it happens in a few months and for others it can take a decade. As such, there is no point in me making promises about how long it will take with This One Easy Trick™. It's not easy, and there is no trick. However, after having hundreds of conversations over the past two years with other career changers, there are patterns as to who does it successfully, and who continues to struggle.

My goal with this book is to share some practical guidelines to help you get started and to form a plan for your own success. Following that plan is, of course, your responsibility.

Depending on your background and your responsibilities, the amount of dedication and learning required could be easy for you or it could be hard. My advice on this is always be realistic about what you can handle and try your best to dedicate uninterrupted time to your progress. I will help you form a learning plan, but only you can work out the logistics of how to fit it into your life. Treat it seriously, and plan it into your calendar like a meeting which can only be cancelled in an emergency.

I have divided this book into three sections, designed to act as a rough guideline for your progress. I am a logical, practical person. As such, I will also try to keep my chapters logical (ie. grounded in reason and experience) and practical (ie. with actionable steps you can take today).

The chapters as a whole are built around a very simple concept that can be summarised as follows:

1. Learn the technical skills
2. Create a network and find a community
3. Find a job by talking to your network about your skills

Of course, there are many ways to achieve these three steps, and I will help guide you as to how you can best achieve them.

Every step on this path requires planning, consistent learning, and constant review and honesty with yourself about how you're progressing and how you can improve. You have already taken the first step by buying this book and reading this introduction, so I know you're ready to learn, self-reflect, and create a plan for success.

Let's get started.

Section 1
What You Need

Developing Your Technical Skills

Changing careers is a risky business. You have to give up part of your life, or at the very least your free time, and dedicate months or years to something that is a massive unknown. It's so easy in this environment to get stuck on yourself: everything you're giving up, everything you want to do, everything you're risking. It's a common way of thinking, but it's also a common pitfall into which I have seen newcomers fall time and again.

Rather than continuously thinking about things from a "me, me, me" perspective, I encourage you to continue trying to reach outside yourself to think about things from another perspective: that of the people hiring you.

Imagine this: you work in recruitment in the HR department of a medium-sized business hoping to expand the number of developers working on their online offering. You already have a good team of around ten developers, but they just can't handle the load anymore. They're stressed out, and management has approved a budget for hiring one more person to spread the work.

The company starts by trying to recruit a senior developer, someone who can jump in immediately to lighten the burden on the existing team. Quickly though, you realise that the few people you can get to interview as seniors are asking for salaries way beyond what's been budgeted. You have to downgrade your expectations, and you end up trying to hire a junior instead. Suddenly, you're inundated with over 100 applications. It's your job to try to find the person who can jump into the most amount of work in the least amount of time but at the budget you want. How do you do it? What do you look for?

This is the everyday life of many recruiters around the world. Change a few variables (e.g., make it a remote, work-from-anywhere job at a top company) and suddenly 100 turns into 1,000.

Competition for junior positions is fierce, and when you think about the above scenario, it's easy to feel discouraged. Like it or not, nine times out of ten the recruiter will choose the 'safe' option to come and interview: someone who's a recent computer science graduate, young and eager to please new bosses, and who has been raised as part of a digital generation.

The important question isn't: 'Is it possible for a (for example) 33-year-old immigrant mum to get a position over these "easy" hires?' We know it's possible because she's writing this book. The question is: "What can you do to stand out enough to grab a recruiter's attention in an environment where they're steering away from risk?'

This is the main point for this section: you represent a risk to hiring managers. You will constantly have to fight to reassure people that you're either worth that risk or not a risk at all. That's the core of your value proposition, and it's what we will aim to build together throughout this book.

However, let me also emphasise this point: there's no point in networking, building a brand, creating a value proposition, or standing out to recruiters if you don't have the technical skills and tools you need. There's a level of proficiency and a way of thinking that you must develop if you're going to build a programming career. That's what this section will explore.

Together, we'll create a solid learning plan which covers choosing and mastering a programming language, developing proficiency in secondary tools, and building impressive projects. At the end of the section, I'll also cover a few options for non-programming careers you can consider if your learning plan leads you to the conclusion that programming isn't for you.

Chapter 1

Learning Mentality

Before we begin, it's important to take a moment to think about how we learn. There are, of course, innumerable books on this topic. Everything from forming micro-habits to the 10,000-hours rule of mastery. This book is not purely about learning, and I'm not a psychologist. However, I do want to familiarise you with three major themes of learning any skill, which might help you to think about how you learn and keep you sane in the process.

Recognition vs Recall

Something you'll see me come back to time and again is the discussion of active vs passive learning. Watching a YouTube video is passive learning, and struggling to code your first to-do-list app is active learning. One is significantly better than the other. I emphasise the importance of building projects and 'getting your hands on the keyboard' because the temptation to engage in passive learning is so strong, particularly in the current generation raised on video content.

The reason I'm such a strong advocate of active learning is because of the concepts of recognition and recall. These two ideas are about how we remember things. Most of our knowledge can be roughly sorted into these two categories.

Recognition is when we hear or see something familiar, and we think 'Oh yes, I know what that is!' An example of this is when we hear a song on the radio that we haven't heard in a long time. 'Oh yeah,' we think. 'I remember this one!' You might even be able to sing along with some of the words.

Recall, on the other hand, is the ability to generate information and knowledge and actively bring it to mind. In the above example, you would probably be unable to recall the lyrics to the song if it hadn't been playing. You didn't even remember the song existed!

As another example, kids raised in bilingual households often report being able to understand a language but not to actively speak it. This is an example of having recognition but not recall.

Similarly, when learning programming (or any skill), it's important to take a moment to consider: 'Am I learning recognition right now, or recall?' In general, passively absorbing information by watching YouTube videos, listening to podcasts, or reading an article will assist in the recognition of terminology, concepts, syntax, etc. It's not useless and it's not wasted time. However, the ability to recall this information in order to solve an actual problem will only come with practice and should, therefore, be prioritised.

Although it might seem foreign to you now, a day will come when you'll need to explain the theory behind the code you write or actively use an algorithmic pattern to solve a tricky problem. You'll need recall in these situations, and that won't come from watching other people code.

ANNA JEAN MCDOUGALL

The Dunning-Kruger Effect

One of the most common patterns of learning involves the Dunning-Kruger effect, renowned in pop culture as the explanation for insufferable beginners. However, the psychological phenomenon itself is helpful for understanding some of the struggles you will go through.

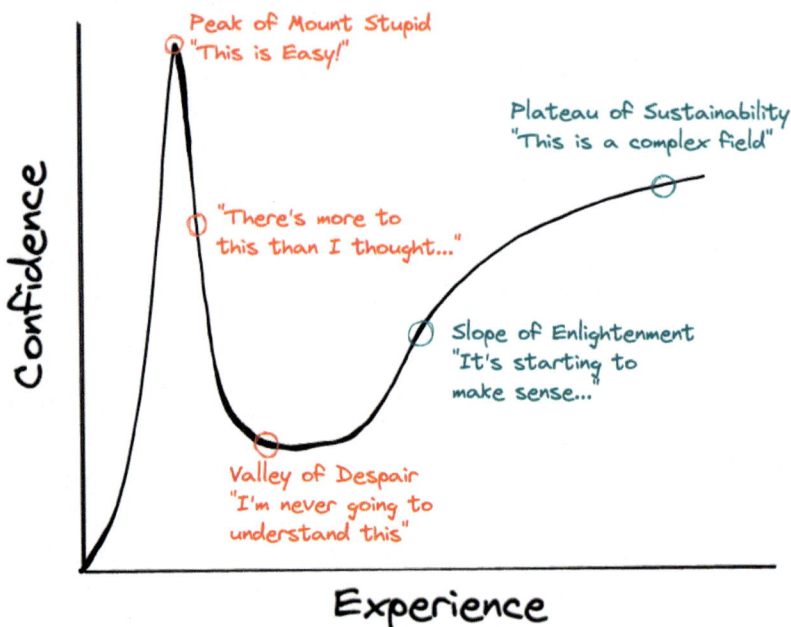

It's hard to conceptualise just how enormous the field of tech is. When you begin, you'll hopefully be so laser-focused on one area that you'll start to think it's easy. It's not. Once you realise this, you'll feel inadequate, hopeless, and totally overwhelmed. This is a perfectly normal feeling, but that doesn't stop it from being extremely unpleasant. Unfortunately, the only way out is to keep going. If you have the fortitude to continue, you'll find that your knowledge slowly builds and you'll overcome the despair you've felt to build a better, more solid understanding of your field.

I'm not saying all this to scare you, but rather to make you aware that going through such a phase, although unpleasant, is normal and expected. If you've ever learned a foreign language or tried to master a sport, then you'll be familiar with the sensation and may be more prepared for it. If this is your first time really trying to become seriously good at a new skill, then this feeling is likely to surprise you and make you doubt your abilities. Please be aware that reaching the valley of despair is a *good sign* and has nothing to do with your intelligence. It means you're starting to see beneath the surface and get to a level where you can begin to comprehend the wider role your skills can play.

Imposter Syndrome

Funnily enough, a lot of my advice for dealing with the Dunning-Kruger effect (and the valley of despair) equally applies to tech's favourite topic: imposter syndrome. By far the most common question I get asked at conferences, meetups, and other events is whether I deal with imposter syndrome and, if so, how I deal with it.

Let's begin by covering what imposter syndrome is.

Imposter syndrome involves the feeling of being woefully inadequate and underprepared for the role or task you have in front of you and, consequently, terrified that someone in a position of authority or expertise will discover you're a fraud. Typically, this goes hand-in-hand with fears of being fired or kicked out of a program.

The common advice you'll receive about imposter syndrome covers a whole bunch of statements that, while accurate and factual, are entirely unhelpful for actually improving the situation. For example:

- 'Everyone feels that way sometimes, even seniors and experts!'
- 'I'm sure you're fine at your job!'

- 'Don't worry about it—the feeling will pass.'

What is far more useful when encountering this feeling (since you almost certainly will) is dealing with the core, underlying beliefs. So, let's break down the above definition of imposter syndrome and try to look at what's actually happening.

Firstly, the feeling that you're inadequate for a task ahead of you implies two things:

1. You should have all the knowledge you need for every task you're given.
2. Being unsure of something is bad.

Both of these statements are categorically untrue. Ask any ballroom dancer or language-learner who their ideal practice partner would be and you're likely to get the same response: 'Someone who is better than me, but not too much better than me'. The same is true for tasks and goals.

Having a task that is outside your current range of knowledge is great! It means you're forced to expand your understanding and continue your own development. Being given tasks or projects where you already know how to do everything sounds like an extremely boring way to live, and it breaks the cardinal rule of tech, which is that everything changes and you must keep learning.

Additionally, software and web development are team sports. If you've ever played a team sport, such as soccer, then you know that a goalkeeper can't also be a star shooter, and the skills a full-back needs are vastly different from either role. Tech is infintesimily larger as a field than soccer, so why would you assume you should be able to take on all those roles? In short, lacking knowledge and being unsure are good things! They force you to expand your skills, talk to other developers, and work out what parts of tech you enjoy and what parts you are happy to leave to other people.

The only caveat to this is when a task is so far outside your field of expertise as to be laughable. If that's the case, then it's a problem from above. There is absolutely nothing wrong with approaching your lead and saying 'This task is outside what I can do'. In fact, it's good for them to hear that so they can properly support you. In the best case scenario, you'll be paired with another developer who can walk you through how to solve a problem. In the worst case scenario, they'll reassign the task. Either way, you win.

The second part of imposter syndrome is the fear of being 'found out', of your supervisor or lead discovering that you are the worst developer in the room. Usually, people who feel this way react by shutting down, shutting up, and suffering in silence. I want to encourage you to do the opposite: open up, pipe up, and suffer publicly.

As stated earlier, common advice surrounding imposter syndrome is that 'everyone feels that way sometimes.' Although the statement itself is mind-bogglingly useless, it is worth noting one of the implications of this, which is that other people understand how you feel. You can openly state: 'This is a bit overwhelming and I am really feeling the imposter vibes right now', and people will leap in to help you because they've been there too. Weirdly enough, drawing attention to your feelings of inadequacy will help you to become a better developer and, therefore, also help you to not feel so inadequate.

Lastly, I want to encourage you to really have a look at what role your ego is playing here. People with imposter syndrome often say: 'I feel like the worst developer in the room', and all the onlookers will jump in to reassure them it's not true. But...What if it is true? What if you are the worst developer in the room?

I would argue that being the worst developer in the room is an opportunity. It means you're surrounded by people who you can learn from. If you can take the 'fear of judgement' mindset and turn it into a 'learning opportunity' mindset, you will find imposter syndrome significantly easier to deal with.

ANNA JEAN MCDOUGALL

Think of a scenario in which you're really good at something, let's say baking. You're a great baker and you go to a meeting of other bakers, and there's someone at the meeting who starts to zone out and look really despondent. You talk to them and they say: 'I just feel like I don't belong here... I've burned all the bread I've tried to make.'

How do you feel towards that person? Do you feel angry that they came to the meeting and want to kick them out of the club? I doubt it. More likely, you feel happy that they came to the meeting and told you what was wrong so now you and the other expert bakers can improve their baking.

You have to let go of the fear of being the worst in the room. So, you burn all your code every time you try to bake it—great! Now you have a problem you can bring to your meeting and talk about with the other developers. If there's one thing developers love, it's a problem!

You might very well be the worst in the room, and that's fine! Embrace it, lean into it, open up about it, and you might find that, one month later, you're feeling a lot more confident about everything that concerned you before.

Chapter 2

What Skills, Tools, or Programming Languages Should You Learn?

This is, by far, the most common question I am asked. The simple, albeit frustrating answer is: it depends.

Of course, I won't leave you hanging. The answer 'it depends' naturally leads to 'what does it depend on?' That is the question I will answer in this section. Later in this section, I will also cover the step-by-step process for how to learn these things.

Essential Skill #1: A Programming Language

Before I begin giving you guidelines for which languages are used for which purposes, a small proviso: choosing one of these doesn't 'lock you in' to that programming language or that area of development for the rest of your life.

Time and again, I hear beginner coders say: 'I'm learning Python, JavaScript, and Java because I want to be a full stack developer but I have an interest in machine learning.' Well, yes… JavaScript and Java are good full stack languages to have, and Python is particularly well-loved and well-used in the area of machine learning. However, trying to learn three programming languages at once is like trying to learn Portuguese, Italian, and Spanish all at the same time. They're similar enough that you'll get it all mixed up in your head, be unable to keep each one straight, and end up failing to do any of them particularly well.

The simple truth is this: the broad majority of programming languages use similar logical concepts, vocabulary, and syntax. If you can learn one programming language very well, you can learn other languages much faster at a later date. To continue with the same analogy, if you become fluent in Spanish, then, later on, learning Italian will be much easier. You might still get a few words mixed up, but the end result will be that you can become fluent in both.

In general, these are the programming languages that I usually recommend to newcomers, in no particular order:

- JavaScript: websites, applications, front-end, UI/UX, servers
- Java: servers, software, working with databases
- Python: machine learning, data science, artificial intelligence

In my mind, these are the 'big three' of programming today. However, if for whatever reason these don't interest you, you can try some of these out:

- C++, C#, C, or Unity: game development
- Ruby, Ruby on Rails
- Swift
- Flutter
- Kotlin
- Go

These languages will all give you a solid foundation, but are not as commonly sought after and might be a bit more 'niche'. The 'C-suite' languages of the first bullet point are common but also notoriously hard as first programming languages, so only dive into one of those if you're up for a challenge.

Essential Skill #2: An Integrated Developer Environment (IDE) or 'Code Editor'

I remember that when I started learning to code, I was totally overwhelmed by the amount of acronyms and jargon I encountered. 'IDE' is one of the most common, and it stands for 'integrated development environment'. When I first played around with HTML as a kid, IDEs weren't something I came across; you simply opened Notepad or Word and saved the document as '.html' instead of '.doc' or '.txt' and 'Voila!' you had a website. Funnily enough, you can still do that, but some smart engineers somewhere decided that the experience could be a lot more enjoyable.

IDEs are really just 'code editors'; think of them as Microsoft Word for programming. Sure, Notepad (or any basic text editor) can take down words just as easily as Word can, but Word comes with some other features that make it more attractive: spelling checker, word count, templates, etc.

Similarly, IDEs provide a range of features (as well as plugins) to make the experience of developing code far easier. For example, there are plugins that automatically format what you write, reload your webpage every time you change your code, and allow you to create 'template' code based on what you're doing.

As someone new to programming, a lot of these things might seem totally foreign and unnecessary at this point, but these skills can save you a lot of time in the long-run, especially if you dedicate a few minutes in each programming session to learning a new keyboard shortcut.

In general, which IDE you use will depend on two things:

1. What programming language are you using?
2. What is your personal preference?

Try doing a search for your programming language and 'IDE' and see what your options are. Most popular programmes will enable you to do a lot of similar things, and there is rarely a right or wrong answer. Even in the professional workplace, most companies will let you use whichever editor you prefer.

Once you've picked an editor, keep a copy of its shortcuts near you (some people print them out and stick them on the wall, others have them as computer backgrounds or laminated posters) and try to use them regularly. Look into the most common plugins for your programming language and challenge yourself to try to use them. Most of the time, these minor improvements will feel clunky and weird at first but will end up streamlining your development in the long-term and are also good tools to have up your sleeve before entering job interviews. The sooner you start to learn and practice them, the easier they will be!

Essential Skill #3: Basic Command Line

You'll hear many different terms for the command line as soon as you begin developing: the terminal, the shell, bash, and the console. For the sake of learning as a beginner, you can see these terms as more or less interchangeable. The most important thing is that command line skills allow you to navigate and control your computer via the keyboard.

Most likely, you are totally at home with using what's called the graphical user interface (GUI) to do basic computer tasks. For example, to create a new file you probably select 'File > New', or to copy a file you might right-click it and select 'Copy'. The command line enables you to do these things without having to click, select, or use any shortcuts.

Why would you need to do this? Because often in programming, you're already using the terminal or command line to run your programme, save your files using Git (see next skill below), or install new add-ons. You can, of course, do all that in the command line and then stop, click into your files, right-click, select copy, click into another folder, and paste…but it is significantly longer than just typing the command directly into the terminal.

One thing I'll keep coming back to in this book is that programmers are lazy. By that I mean that when we see an opportunity to streamline or automate something, we take it. It might seem like a lot of work to learn a bunch of new commands just to navigate your computer, but, in the end, it

29

saves future-you from having to click away and break out of your programming environment. Long-term it's a beautiful, lazy skill to have.

Take some time to learn how to do the following with the command line:

- Work out which folder you're in now
- Browse to another folder
- Go up a level in the folder tree
- Create a new file
- Copy a file
- Move a file
- Read the contents of a text file
- Open a new file in your IDE

On this last point, most IDEs also have terminals/consoles. I usually write my programmes with the console open the entire time. If you can get to the point of reducing the amount of clicking and selecting you do and instead shift to doing most tasks via the keyboard, you'll save time and also look super cool.

PRO TIP: Speaking of looking super cool, make sure to use the black background with green text for your console, then all your friends will think you're hacking the Matrix.

Essential Skill #4: Version Control

If you already know what 'Git' or 'GitHub' are, then feel free to skip this section. If you read the last sentence and think 'Uhhh what?' then read on.

Version control is a super cool thing that allows multiple people to work on the same code at the same time. It's highly necessary, used (almost) everywhere, and is a skill often overlooked by those teaching themselves at home simply because they don't have to collaborate with anyone other than themselves.

If you're working alone on your own pet project, then all you need is an IDE and the 'save' button. However, the moment you start working on code with others (be it for practice or professionally), version control comes into play.

Simply put, version control keeps track of all the changes you (and others) make to your code, and allows you all to work on it at the same time without the risk of losing progress, accidentally overwriting someone else's work, or having your code clash.

For example, imagine I'm working with my friend Lewes on a Facebook-like application. My task is to allow users to upload multiple photos and Lewes's job is to allow users to upload video files. In a non-version-controlled world, we would both download the same 'starting code', complete our tasks, and then send back the finished code.

However, what if I change some core logic when allowing multiple photo uploads? I send back my code, but it clashes with Lewes's version allowing video uploads. Either my version is loaded, or his is, or one of us has to go through the code line-by-line to find all the changes and create a third version that has both sets of changes. Yikes!

Version control avoids the above scenario by separating out or 'branching' off from the main code for each task. When one task is done, it's integrated back into the main codebase (usually called the 'main branch') and then Lewes can either manually or automatically pull those changes into his own code while he's still working on his task, creating the 'third version' we mentioned earlier just by typing one command into his terminal. Of course, Lewes should still review my code to see if there are any clashes or if he can (re)use any of the logic I wrote, but he doesn't need to worry about accidentally removing my feature or losing his own.

In addition to all of the above, something I haven't touched on at all is the sheer size of a professional codebase. Unlike personal projects, which could be as small as three files, the majority of professional codebases are behemoths, which can't easily be tracked or emailed back and forth amongst team members. Version control also helps us avoid the problem of multiple downloads, installations of different versions, or the inevitable 'working from an old version' problem that can easily happen when emailing documents back and forth.

To learn version control, you'll have to learn how to do the following things in Git, the leading version control tool in the industry:

- Clone: copying existing code repositories.
- Add: adding changes to a 'version' in a pending state.
- Commit: committing (or 'saving') changes to a version.
- Pull: 'pulling in' the latest version of the code.
- Push: 'pushing up' your changes to the code.
- Branch: 'branching off' from the main code with a feature, bug fix, or similar.
- Merge: merging changes from one branch to another.

These are the absolute basics for a beginner programmer to address. In addition, it is a good idea to become familiar with some of the online tools for managing or 'cloudifying' Git repositories. The two biggest names in this space as of writing are GitHub and GitLab.

GitHub is the 'assumed' tool of choice for those learning to code and has the added benefit of being able to host web applications, provide profile pages, and have communities where you can ask questions.

GitLab seems to be more tailored toward professional usage, so it could be good to use later in your learning if you have some sort of team/group assignment and just want to try out a new tool but, otherwise, GitHub will give you all the skills you need.

One final note: learn these skills early and use them often. Many developers have a 'Git cheat sheet' near their workspaces. It's worth trying to use proper Git commands even when working alone because a lot of these concepts take time to sink in but are much easier to remember when put into practice.

Essential Skill #5: Searching the Internet

I can almost see your eyebrows raising as you read this, but give me a chance here.

I've already mentioned a few mistakes I see new developers make in their thinking, but there is one more major one that comes up time and again: trying to memorise code.

Let me write two sentences, and I want you to read them (ideally out loud) ten times before you move on: "There is nothing wrong with searching the internet. Programming is about problem solving, not memorisation."

Remember how I mentioned that programming languages all work on similar principles? That's part of why this is true: because how you think as a programmer is more important than what you type. Rather than trying to memorise syntax for programming languages (e.g. how to write a loop), focus on understanding the concepts of programming languages (e.g. what is a loop and when should I use one?). Also, notice that I didn't say 'memorise' the concepts. That's because those, too, can be looked up again later.

For example, in JavaScript there's 'slice' and 'splice'. I have literally created YouTube videos covering these two methods and yet I still cannot tell you which is which because I always mix them up. I use Google or Ecosia every single time I need one of these methods or see them in someone else's code. That doesn't make me a bad developer because memorising syntax or methods is not what makes a good developer. A lot of memorisation will happen naturally over time and with practice, but the truth is that a huge proportion of professional development work involves searching online for others who have solved similar problems.

As another example, here is a meme I shared early in my time in programming, which got a huge response:

Stack Overflow is one of many websites you'll come across where programming questions have been asked and answered. This meme resonated with a lot of developers because we're constantly using search engines and Stack Overflow to help us with tricky programming problems. I probably run about 100+ searches every single day that I work.

Now that we've clarified that searching is an absolutely essential part of development, and that memorisation is not, I hope that it's become clear why improving your search skills is worth doing. Look into the various ways you can run searches, how to search for particular sources (e.g. Stack Overflow), how to exclude search results with certain terms, etc. These skills are easy to develop (I'd say two to three YouTube videos or blog posts would be all you need) and highly effective at getting you to your solutions more quickly.

Chapter 3

How Can I Learn Programming Given My Life Circumstances?

This is, potentially, the main reason you decided to buy this book. You know you're interested in programming. You know you need to learn it. Now, you even know the additional skills and tools that are good to have under your belt. But how do you fit this into your life? How do you go from zero to technically proficient?

Well…'It depends'!

Some people reading this will be students leaving high school, looking for a profession. Some will be parents in their 30s or 40s coming out of parental leave, looking for a pathway back into work. Some will be full-time workers at a supermarket, looking for a way to be more financially stable while still putting in their hours.

On top of that, this book is likely to have readers from every continent on the planet, from families rich and poor, and from backgrounds ranging from the highly technically competent (e.g. kids who had computers in their living rooms or even their bedrooms) to those who only recently became computer literate.

As a result, I'm going to focus on options: what options are available; how much time/focus those options take; and how any person reading this book can set solid, realistic goals for reaching technical competence. Naturally, what's offered will vary from city to city, state to state, and country to country. Hopefully, you'll find at least two options available to you so you can choose, but it may be that only one way is possible for you to undertake.

Options for Learning Programming in Person (*at least traditionally!)

There's a saying that when choosing a service, you should consider three factors: speed, quality, and price. You can choose any two of these, but you'll never get all three. Depending on your life circumstances, you should take a moment now to consider which is most important to you. There's no right or wrong answer here, it's entirely up to you and your circumstances.

Speed

When considering speed, you should be thinking about how soon you want to transition into tech. Most people reading this will probably be thinking 'as soon as possible', but remember that how quickly the job search pays off for you will also depend on the time you invest not only into learning the skills but also into networking and growing your online and/or in-person presence. However, there are some situations where speed is of the utmost importance, and this is usually tied to situations you want to escape, such as joblessness, homelessness, a bad family environment, or a toxic workplace. Sometimes the speed of the escape really is the most important factor, and if that's your situation, then you should prioritise this factor.

Quality

Quality is one of the considerations most people *think* they want but which can hide a few pitfalls as well. The upsides are obvious: the higher the quality of what you learn, the more thorough you can be, the better you can know your options, and the more likely you are to pass a technical interview and write good code. However, there's also a level to which the quality of training will never prepare you for the real-world applications of your skills. Simply put: practice is the best way to learn, and the quality of learning in the following options—although important—will not necessarily make you a good programmer in the same way practice can. That said, if you're in a comfortable position in life and have time and/or money easily available, then quality should absolutely be your top consideration.

Price

Most people love a bargain. Why pay thousands of dollars for a years-long programme if you can get Harvard Computer Science 101 for free online? I get it. For many people, paying that money is not even an option without some sort of scholarship or external funding. There are also many online courses, for example, that balance price and quality marvellously. But, in general, the price you can afford is highly dependent on your life circumstances and is not a simple matter of preference. If, however, you're lucky enough to have savings to burn in your bank account, then you can let this priority go and focus on quality and time instead.

This section will cover six options for learning, each with massive pros and cons. I'll spend most of the time focusing on options for online learning, since there are many sub-options available which you can look into.

Option 1: University Degree Programmes

Speed: 2-6 years
Quality: High
Price: Varies by country

There are many different degrees that include programming skills, but the typical degree you'll see developers hold is a BSc in Computer Science. You'll see this referred to as a 'CS degree' throughout most of this book and online. It's important, however, to note that, as technology expands into different areas and professions, the number and type of degrees supporting that expansion increases. For example, there are degrees in cybersecurity, machine learning, data science, and more.

The clear, knock-you-over-the-head obvious upside of a degree is having the piece of paper. By completing the many years required to obtain your qualifications, employers are quick to interview you. The time (and often financial) investment you have already made into learning about computing represents a reduction in risk. Simply put: employers see you as a sure bet because they know many people skilled in computing (your professors) have already evaluated your abilities and given you grades based on them. From the employer's perspective, this means you have already passed many small technical interviews before you even walk through the door. Who wouldn't be interested in that?

In addition, completing a degree does allow you the time to truly dig into the subject area and become an 'expert' if you so desire. A CS degree, in particular, will expose you to many different areas of computing and give you time to work on those areas, see what you like/dislike, and discover which area should be your focus. This is in contrast to faster methods, which often lead to you working in programming for a very long time. It's much harder to change focusses away from programming if you find it's not for you later, and the nature of full-time work also means you're less likely to be able to explore those other areas once employed.

One thing which is important to mention here is that a CS degree is almost always focused on theory: how systems work, what the cloud is, what security vulnerabilities are, various algorithms/calculus, etc. Believe it or not, there's often very little practical application of programming within these degrees. On the whole, most CS degrees include one to three courses on programming itself. If you know for a fact that programming is what you want to do, then I would recommend you look into other options. If, however, you want a broad understanding of systems and technologies, which will set you up for multiple possible career paths, then this could be a good option.

Of course, the downside is time. If you want results or need a new career quickly, this is not the option for you. Additionally, most countries have steep fees for a degree. It is entirely possible that you're not someone who can support those fees.

If you're cash-poor in a high-cost education country but really think a degree is right for you in all other ways, don't despair just yet. It's worth contacting your local universities to look into scholarships. The best thing you can do is to pick up the phone (I know, I know) and call any university you would be open to attending and speak directly to the scholarships office. Tell them your situation and ask if there are options for you. If you're part of any sort of historically excluded group, you may also find non-profit organisations or philanthropists who want to help you out. Mention those statuses to the scholarships office as well. Scholarship applications can take time and effort but, because of that, relatively few people apply to many of them. Just applying might get you ahead.

Of course, some people within well-connected communities will also try crowdfunding. Or maybe it's time you called that distant relative who you heard is doing well. However you go about it, take the time to truly look into all your options if it's something you want. If, after all that research and all those applications, you're still not able to attend, never fear, there are other options we'll look at. You can still have a career in tech!

Option 2: Apprenticeships and Company-Run Training Programmes

Speed: 2-3 years
Quality: Varies
Price: Unpaid or you get a small income

If you have little to no interest in mathematics or theory but know for a fact that you want to work as a developer, then take a moment to read this through carefully.

In some countries, such as my new home of Germany, there are apprenticeship programmes. They provide an amazing opportunity, especially if you don't require a 'living' income. By that, I mean you have a partner who can support you, are still living with your parents, or have enough savings to fund your lifestyle.

An apprenticeship is really quite straightforward: you work full-time for a company, but they hire you knowing that you have no experience. What you receive is training in your chosen profession and (usually) a small income. What they receive is an employee who is, at first, a liability (you provide very little value and are paid) but who will eventually be a real money-maker. By the end of your training, you should provide a lot of value but still be paid very little.

How these programmes work is largely dependent upon the local laws/regulations, as well as the quality of the company you work for. As an example, here in Germany, an apprenticeship in tech normally lasts for 3 years, pays between 800 and 1200 Euros per month (as of writing), and is performed in conjunction with some sort of learning institution that helps with training. For someone straight out of high school or who has a supplementary income, this is adequate. For those who are already living independently, who have full-time work, or have kids to look after, this may not be possible. As a point of comparison, Glassdoor reports that the average income of a software engineer in Germany was about 2,800 Euros a month after tax in 2021.

Nevertheless, I'm of the opinion that this is a pretty good deal. You learn the ropes, get a lot of practical experience for your CV, and get paid for the whole thing. It's important to note, however, that this is absolutely a full-time job and must be treated that way. Do not try to hold a second job while you do this. Not only will it burn you out in terms of time and energy, but you won't have the mental rest required to adequately store what you learn. This last point is crucial because, if you're learning well, then you will (and should) be tired at the end of the day. Sleep will be your best friend for consolidating that knowledge and building upon it.

The other caveat here is that this system is not available in every country, and many countries partake in dubious, multi-year 'work experience' or 'internship' programmes that are completely unpaid and totally exploitative. It's up to you to decide if this on-the-job learning is the best method for you and, if so, how much/little you're willing to get for the effort and time you put in.

One other note of warning is that this system has the potential to fail you big-time. The wrong company, the wrong supervisor, or the wrong learning path will see you flounder and be left clueless.

For this reason, I would always advise following some of the steps/suggestions for self-learning in this book prior to accepting an apprenticeship or traineeship. Any sort of head start you can get will help you significantly, especially if you're someone who gets nervous with pressure or finds yourself eager to please new employers. It is also possible that the program has a probation period of two to six months, and making it through that probation is essential if you really want to see out the entire training period.

Done properly, however, apprenticeships/traineeships will see you emerge from the cocoon a fully formed programming butterfly. You may be offered a full-time position by the company you train with or, if you didn't enjoy that work environment, you'll be in a great position to find another job. Better yet, if you heed the rest of the advice in this book, you'll find that the people and business skills you learn in these few years will pay huge dividends in terms of career prospects upon finishing.

Option 3: Boot Camp

Speed: 3-6 months
Quality: Low (see more below)
Price: Free to $15,000 (usually with funding support or scholarship options)

Boot Camps are one of the big, booming subsectors of the tech economy. Boot camp operators can see the talent gap in tech and the throngs of people wanting to get in on it. As a result, they came up with a good system for making money: teach the fundamentals of programming quickly, pipeline those students into jobs, and charge a lot of money for it.

Boot camps end up being controversial because a lot of people already in tech either love or hate them, and a lot of boot camp operators are either great at what they do or give the entire boot camp industry a less-than-desirable reputation. Personally, I think boot camps are a good thing, both for students and for tech, but there are many ways they could be better.

Let's start with the most obvious benefit of a boot camp: time saved. If you're someone who needs to get into tech yesterday, and you can afford to put three months aside, you can complete one of these courses and reasonably expect to get interviews at the end of it. Those three months will be full of extremely intense, non-stop learning. You won't have time to hang out with friends, take a breather with your family, or work even a casual job.If that's your plan, scratch it out right now. Every single bootcamp graduate I've spoken to has described their experience as 'intense' or 'a whirlwind'. It's three months where you accept that you'll have no other life, and you dive headfirst into it in the hope that you will learn a lot and emerge hired. In some situations, that's exactly what happens.

Another not-so-obvious benefit of (good) boot camps is that they connect well with local businesses hiring in your area. In fact, if you're choosing to go the boot camp route, *the* deciding factor for which one you pick should be the company's networking opportunities.

Here are some questions you can ask a boot camp operator to establish this:

- 'What networking events do you have with employers?'
- 'Do you have a dedicated staff member for connecting employers with graduates?'
- 'What percentage of your graduates get a tech job within six months of finishing?'
- 'What local companies do you work closely with?'

Almost all boot camps will teach you a lot of basics extremely fast and leave you gasping for air, but at the end of the day, it's the company's networking opportunities that allow you to take advantage of that knowledge or not. As you'll see in later chapters, forming networks and finding contacts who know you beyond your coding ability is usually the deciding factor between who gets hired and who doesn't. With that in mind, it's worth prioritising these potential connections in your search.

In terms of the cost, there's no denying that boot camps are expensive. It's the singular reason I didn't pursue one and instead took another route (as you'll see later). However, there are two core ways that boot camps have removed (or reduced) this barrier to entry: scholarships and loans.

Boot camp scholarships are usually hard to come by and are reserved for people with significant financial hurdles or burdens. For example, a single parent on a low income, an unemployed person with a strong interest in programming, or a financially disadvantaged person from an historically excluded group. For a cohort of 10-15 students, I usually see boot camps advertise that 2-3 scholarship positions are available. Sometimes, a generous donor will bump that number up, but they remain competitive. As with my advice on degrees, however, I would always encourage you to apply if you meet the criteria. The worst that can happen is they say no, and then you're no worse off than you are now!

The other option is a loan. Normally, boot camps administer loans to anyone who wants one through a third-party provider. If they're being upfront about this, the advertising or website will say something like 'financing options available' or 'payment plans available'. Very often, the advertising will instead say 'FREE*' and the asterisk will tell you that you pay nothing now. If you ever see a boot camp advertised as free, take the time to look into it first. You'll often find it's actually on a loan basis.

How loans are repaid can also vary from boot camp to boot camp, but the most common model is that of repayment based on income. Put simply: you only pay them back once you earn above a certain amount. The idea is, of course, that they're so confident you'll get a job after graduating that they won't force you to repay the loan until you do. When you read this, you're probably thinking 'Well that sounds great!' but just wait a moment before you jump in.

Although the average person, upon seeing the above deal ('Pay us back only after you get a job!'), would assume that 'getting a job' means in the tech sector, it's important to note that this is almost never a requirement. In other words, if you complete the course and return to your hospitality job but earn above the $30,000 threshold (or however much it is), you still have to repay that loan, even though you have not successfully transitioned into a tech career.

On top of that, loans are always tricky and depend a lot on the provider. Always think about the above criteria ('At what point do I have to begin repaying this loan?') as well as the interest/repayment rate ('How much of my income will I have to sacrifice?') and then sit down with a calculator to work out how long it would take to pay it off based on the minimum salary amount. If you're looking at a minimum of 5 years of repaying about 15% of your income each month, is that worth it for you? Would you be left with enough to afford rent/food/etc. in your area?

When doing these calculations, always assume the worst. Knowing the worst-case scenario means you can adequately prepare and then, if/when you're successful (as hopefully this book will help you be!), it can all be a nice big relief that it never came to pass. If you aren't successful in making the switch, then you know what the cost of that is and it won't be a big shock to future-you.

Now that we've covered the basics of how boot camps are funded, let's have a look at the actual content of these courses.

Most boot camps will teach you web development because it's the most accessible in terms of being able to see and understand the results of your programming work immediately. In other words, you programme something and it's immediately available in a browser for you to see. Furthermore, web-based applications are extremely useful; every company needs a website nowadays.

Boot camps are also increasingly offering other paths, such as data science or backend programming. These are great if you already have an interest in the topics, but they're much harder to conceptualise if you don't already have some exposure to the technical landscape. For example, if you don't know what 'backend' is. There's no problem with that, but it's a big part of why these courses tend not to be as popular or as highly available.

For a web development boot camp, the absolute minimum you'll learn is HTML, CSS, and JavaScript. Most likely, they'll also try to teach you something called a 'framework' or a 'library' such as React, Vue, or Angular. The first three languages are all essential if you want to go into web development. A library or framework is good to have before beginning your job search, but you only really need one of them to get started.

Regardless, trying to learn four different technologies/tools in three months is a big ask. This is part of the reason why most boot camp graduates emerge severely underprepared for the job market. Their exposure to the technologies they need to learn (as we covered earlier) is so cursory and under-practised, even with full-time study for three months, that most of them will end up doing internships rather than being hired as juniors. There's nothing wrong with paid internships, of course, but they're not often the dream scenario students are sold by boot camp marketing teams.

Simply put, boot camps are expensive crash courses in programming. Their benefit, from my perspective, is twofold:

1. They force you to learn because you pay a lot of money for them and put the rest of your life on hold, so your motivation is high.
2. Good boot camps connect you to other developers and companies who are looking for junior talent.

One of the major downsides is the fact that you rarely emerge prepared for the job market, and you'll normally have to put in six or more months of self-study, additional project work, and your own networking to get you across the line and into a junior position. That often ends up turning the three-month timeframe into a one- or multi-year timeframe. As someone who transitioned into tech after one year, I think that's still a really great result, but you have to keep this in mind when boot camp websites promise you six-figure incomes with only three months of dedication.

The other downside is burnout. Burnout is a hot topic in the tech community because it happens a lot in the workplace, but simply put, it involves working yourself so hard that you lose all passion and motivation, and you end up simply dreading anything around programming.

With boot camps being extremely intense, fast-paced environments where there's pressure to constantly stay ahead of the curve, these programmes can create a state of anxiety for their participants pretty easily.

Worse still, imagine emerging from a boot camp thinking you've learned everything you need to and then discovering you're still a beginner and will be for the next two to three years. On top of that, tech itself is an industry where you have to constantly learn. In a sense, you're always a beginner. After so long grinding and putting that pressure on yourself to succeed, the realisation that you've barely covered the tip of the iceberg can be incredibly demotivating. One of the upsides of a slower programme is that you often develop better habits and a better understanding of how long it can take to master a skill.

All that said, I still come down on the side of thinking boot camps are a net good. They have also been one of the best options available to those furloughed during the pandemic, and we're now seeing those participants emerging as a unique and more diverse group than we traditionally see coming out of universities. From my perspective, that can only be a good thing; tech is for every type of person, so it should be made by every type of person.

Option 4: Night Courses or Community College

Speed: Short courses (6 weeks) to year-long certifications
Quality: Varies (see below)
Price: Low

I'm going to talk briefly about this topic because I rarely see it discussed, but it does often cross over with boot camps nowadays. Most countries have some form of vocational education centre or community college, a low-cost institution with individual 'hobby' courses or longer courses of study with certifications at the end. In Germany, it's Volkshochschule, and in Australia it's TAFE.

Regardless of what it's called, these institutions are beginning to offer more programming courses as part of their standard line-up. Due to the huge variation in offerings, there really isn't much for me to say here except to go and look. See what's available.

At worst, there will be a short programming course for beginners that will give you a taste of web development or a programming language. At best, there will be year-long certifications available. See what's available in your area and if there's a nice way to get started available to you.

Options for Self-Learning Online

It's time to crack your knuckles, sit down with a nice warm drink, and get started on what's sure to be one of the key things you came here to read about: online self-learning.

There's a huge variety of quality information available online, and here I'll endeavour to cover the best and worst aspects of the online world as it comes to learning programming. A summary would be that you usually get what you pay for, but there are some notable exceptions which are free or very low-cost.

The only area I won't be covering here is online boot camps, as they are almost indistinguishable from in-person boot camps. If you haven't yet read *Option 3: Boot camp*, I recommend going back and reading that before continuing.

The biggest issues you'll have if you decide to self-learn with online options are threefold:

1. Motivation
2. Consistency
3. Community

These three things are almost entirely taken care of when you have a structured course of learning. When it comes to creating your own schedule and setting your own goals, however, it can be easy to slip because nobody is holding you accountable. There's also no big bill for you to look at and think 'Well I can't let that go to waste!'

Luckily for you, these three elements will all be covered in this book, at least at a basic level. The first two topics (motivation and consistency) will be integrated into your learning plan later in this section. The third (community) will be covered in section two.

Option 1: Video Platforms

Let's begin with one of the most common ways to learn to code: online video platforms. The two 'big ones' at the time of writing are YouTube and Twitch. YouTube, in particular, is packed full of introductory videos, code-along tutorials, longer programming language courses, and more. Put simply, if you pick any of the recommended tools or programming languages I've mentioned in this book, you'll find innumerable videos designed to help you learn them. Twitch tend towards live video, like real-time code-along sessions, for example, which has the added ability to take questions from viewers.

Let's begin with why this is awesome: it's free, it's convenient, and it's highly accessible. Anyone with an internet connection can learn, for example, what Git is, what it's used for, and how to implement it.

The broad majority of video creators on Twitch and YouTube (myself included) are also doing it as a passion rather than as a profession; it takes a lot of subscribers and watch hours to earn an income on YouTube. What this means is that you'll find plenty of content creators who just want to help you learn as best you can. This is, of course, great…Do you feel the 'however' coming?

However, I maintain that 99.99% of content on YouTube (and Twitch) is best used as a source of supplementary learning material rather than core learning material.

The reason for treating video platforms as supplementary material goes back to my list of three things that make self-learning hard: motivation, consistency, and community. When I evaluate options for self-learning, these are the benchmarks I use to decide whether or not the average person is likely to succeed. YouTube provides no feedback to you about whether or not you're doing well and provides little recourse to get help when you're stuck, which impacts motivation. Consistency isn't supported because the transient nature of YouTube videos (a 'long' video is considered to be one hour and most videos are around ten to twelve minutes) means that you're unlikely to be able to form any sort of schedule around YouTube content. Community is partially assisted with features like live streams, but if you live in an unpopular timezone or have family responsibilities, you could easily miss every live session your tutor of choice has to offer.

In addition to this, one of the things you'll see me emphasise when we get to creating your learning plan is that nothing can replace fingers on a keyboard. Put simply: practice is the key to improving your programming ability. Video platforms provide you with the illusion of learning; you watch a video, you understand what they say, and you think you've learned it. Worse still is when you watch a tutorial, you follow/copy what they do in the tutorial, and it works at the end. You think 'Yay I did it!', but you didn't actually partake in the *core learning* you needed to do, which is problem solving. The tutor has already solved the problems for you and you've just copied.

The biggest hurdle when learning to program is almost always the mental challenge of compartmentalising problems, breaking them down into small steps, and then selecting the tools you need out of your programming language to solve each step. By passively copying solutions, you have a good chance to see how another programmer thinks, but it doesn't actually develop the skills you need to solve it yourself. Again, this is supplementary learning, not core learning.

Furthermore, and I may be speaking mostly for myself here, but there have been plenty of times where I have watched these kinds of tutorials and not even coded along, simply observed. This is the most useless way to 'learn' because everything you see is likely to be erased from your memory by the following week.

So, now that I've eviscerated learning with video platforms, let me tell you how best you *can* learn from them if you decide this is really the best method for you.

How to Learn from a Video Tutorial:

1. Watch the introduction to the video to see what the problem is and to get any of the source code they offer.

2. Stop the video there and then try to solve the problem yourself.

3. Regardless of whether you solve the problem yourself or not, start the video again and watch it all the way through once to see how they solve it.

4. Watch the video again, this time pausing as you go. Pause after every major sentence or idea. The goal is to understand exactly what is being said at every step. Use a search engine for any terms you don't know and only move on once you understand everything.

5. While watching the second time, code along with each step and take the time to comprehend what every line of code is doing, not just generally (e.g. 'this line of code generates a random number') but specifically (e.g. 'Math.random generates a random number between zero and one, we multiply that by the top number we want, and Math.floor then rounds it down to the nearest whole number').

6. Once you've completed the whole video/tutorial in this way, delete all the code you just wrote.

7. Rewrite the solution without the video. You can still use search engines to help you find the commands you need (e.g. 'I know I need to round this number down, but I can't remember what it's called to do that')

8. Once you're done, check your solution against the solution of the video.

a) Is the code the same?
b) If not, how are they different?
c) Do any differences in the code lead to differences in the result of the application?
d) If so, why?
e) If not, could one code be considered better/worse than the other if they produce the same result? What other things might be different instead (e.g. speed, readability, memory usage, etc.)?

The above method is tough. It's designed that way. In my opinion, pre-recorded videos enable our laziness and are great at giving us the illusion of learning. The above methodology is what will lead you to *actually* learn something because it forces you to:

1. Solve the problem yourself using the tools you already have
2. Get your fingers on the keyboard and try to recall methods/functions you have recently encountered
3. Think about different solutions and the benefits/drawbacks of different approaches

Personally, I would much prefer an interactive course and an active community where I can ask questions when I get stuck, get guidance from others, and quickly access reference material (e.g. documentation, which we'll discuss later). If you feel the same, keep reading. There are other ways!

Option 2: Free Courses

I'm not the first person to notice the problems with video platforms as a source of learning. Luckily, some folks with a lot more initiative have come up with a way to offer the benefits of free learning along with the structure and support of a real course.

Free online courses come in many shapes and sizes and, of course, vary drastically in quality. Rather than trying to provide 'general guidelines' as I have for other sections here, I'll instead do some quick case studies on two of the most popular free courses available online now.

Naturally, there are dozens more than just these two, however, these examples will give you a good insight into the basic, free structures available out there. Many other free courses can only be fully unlocked with a full or premium version. Although the prices for these 'freemium' sites can seem steep at first—if you have had a good experience in the free trial, vibe with the instructor(s), and respond well to the method of learning—then it is worth considering paying. Chances are that the costs are far below a boot camp, and if certificates and live learning aren't of utmost importance to you, then it could definitely be worth the cost.

With that said, let's have a look into two of the 'big guns' out there in the world of completely-free online courses.

FreeCodeCamp

No 'learn to code' book would be complete without mentioning the behemoth that is freeCodeCamp. Any search for free coding resources will likely lead you to their website over and over again. There's a good reason for that: freeCodeCamp is one of the best places to dip your toes into the water of programming.

FreeCodeCamp provides step-by-step courses for different 'tracks' of learning, such as web development, machine learning, backend/APIs, data visualisation, application security, and more. Each track is broken down into small sections where you learn one core concept or method and immediately apply it in a web environment. What that means is that you don't need to use your own IDE, Git, or similar software.

The upside of this is that it is extremely accessible and easy to get started. Myself and many others began by trying out a few lessons on freeCodeCamp (or even completing a whole course) and seeing if it was something we enjoyed. They also have a forum where you can ask for help, providing you with a community to lean on. Additionally, there are often suggestions for ways you can combine what you learn into small projects (which you could then ask for feedback in the forums!), and the courses themselves offer 'certificates'.

However, on this last point, it's important to note that very few employers would place significant value on freeCodeCamp certificates, as they're really certificates of completion; no analysis, review, or mentoring occurs to truly note if your result is 'good' or not. This is great as a source of self-motivation—most freeCodeCamp courses run for 300 hours each, so completing one *is* a big achievement!—but it's also important to keep in perspective that freeCodeCamp is (and always should be) used as a stepping stone toward developing with your own IDE.

In my opinion, we're extremely lucky as a community to have access to freeCodeCamp. The only downside is that, for the most part, freeCodeCamp feeds you learning in such small pieces that the solutions to problems are often obvious. I have often had newbie coders say to me: 'I enjoyed freeCodeCamp and found it really great—but I find I can't remember much of it now that it's done.' This is because a lot of the courses were built to help you learn individual tools, but it's only through combining these tools (i.e. by undertaking the projects and reviewing the steps you've just been through) that you can really start to understand how to solve problems with them yourself. Similarly to watching YouTube videos, passively working through a freeCodeCamp course will not allow you to learn nearly as much as you might think.

Naturally, I have some suggestions to help counteract that!

First of all, I would recommend pausing after every ten or so steps in your freeCodeCamp course, reviewing them, and then trying to rewrite a section of code *from scratch* using those concepts. It doesn't need to be perfect, it just needs to be something new that challenges you to combine some of the individual pieces you've learned.

Secondly, I would *always* recommend completing the projects at the end. You'll have to refer back to the material, use a search engine, and potentially even ask for help, but that's fine! The goal is to learn how to problem solve using the tools freeCodeCamp has provided you with.

Thirdly, be sure to 'submit' your solutions to people who can give you real feedback on them. For example, you might post your portfolio on the freeCodeCamp forum, post a little JavaScript game on Twitter, or even share two ways of solving a problem on LinkedIn to ask which is best. There are many different ways to get qualified feedback, but it is an absolutely necessary step, and the sooner you do it, the better. We'll talk more about Questions and Feedback in Chapter 2, but suffice it to say that this is, in itself, a skill you need to learn.

The Odin Project

The Odin Project is essentially an entirely free study program, structured, in many ways, like a boot camp or university course. The curriculum can be scanned in advance but mostly revolves around the classic HTML/CSS/JavaScript web development trio. In addition, the course endeavours to get you started on a framework/library and to dip your toes in the backend. Best of all, before you start any of those things, it introduces you to Linux, the command line, and Git/version control. As you might remember from earlier in the section, these are all skills I recommend learning alongside programming, and the Odin Project hand delivers them to you.

Each unit is structured to begin with theory and end with practice. In the theory section, you'll be presented with text describing the knowledge you need. In addition, there will be additional reading/viewing to supplement that core knowledge, some required, and some optional (like extra credit at school).

Once you feel like you 'get it', you move on to practice. You're presented with a challenge of some sort, and you have to complete it using the knowledge you just acquired. Usually, these challenges are not small, trivial tasks. Instead, they're projects like 'Build an Etch a Sketch game' or 'Create a clone of the Google homepage.' In this way, you're likely to spend more time actually practising your skills than passively taking in information.

Beyond the benefits of this approach, there are two major selling points for the Odin Project that go above and beyond the bare necessities:

1. <u>Community</u>: The Discord community is free, anonymous (if you want), and full of other students going through the curriculum. In addition, you'll find many 'graduates' of the program are still in the forums ready to help if (when) you get stuck.

2. <u>Technological independence</u>: The Odin Project teaches you project setup, live preview, Git, command line, and more. This means that, unlike with freeCodeCamp or Scrimba, you learn how to use your own computer to program in the same way a professional developer does. This is, of course, harder to get started with. In the long-term, though, it can put you a cut above the rest.

Furthermore, the Odin Project allows you to learn how to contribute to open-source projects. You may have heard of 'open source' but have no idea what it means. If so, don't worry about it too much. All you need to know right now is that it's a great skill to have that allows you to engage with the development community and contribute to the building of real-world applications. Since the Odin Project is completely free and itself open-source, they often open up small tasks for beginners to complete.

I could go on and on about how amazing the Odin Project is because it's how I learned web development, and I am definitely biassed in their favour. As of writing, my YouTube channel's most-watched video is me ranting about how great it is! However, it would be remiss of me not to cover some of the drawbacks and the situations in which the Odin Project might not be the best choice for you.

There are four types of people who shouldn't use the Odin Project:

1. If you just want a small sample of programming to see if you like it, then the challenge of setting up a 'developer environment' might be too much for you. To my mind, the Odin Project is perfect for people who already know that they want to do programming and, therefore, want to learn the ins and outs extremely well. It's not as good for people just looking to give it a quick try on the weekend.

2. If you dislike reading and find it a cumbersome exercise, then the Odin Project isn't for you. Most of the units are built around written texts and the recommended materials mostly consist of detailed blog posts or documentation. If you find that you learn far better from visual or aural material, then check out the next course.

3. If you need a certification or some sort of proof 'on paper', the Odin Project doesn't offer that.

4. If you like having a central authority figure to guide you, then the Odin Project is also probably not the best choice. Although there are Discord moderators, the program is community-built and community-run entirely by volunteers. There's no 'big boss' decision-maker or guide. There's also no mentoring, although I personally found a quasi-mentor through the Discord forums purely by asking a lot of questions and opening up discussions with some of the moderators about their recommendations.

Personally, I used the Odin Project for two months before I switched to an in-person course, which offered me the official paperwork and government support I needed. Those two months of pre-study prepared me for the first six months of my course, which is part of why I feel so confident in the quality being offered. Many of the skills I learned through the Odin Project I now use every day.

Overall, the Odin Project is another resource that is invaluable to our community. The Discord channel, in particular, was partly responsible for convincing me I would be welcome in tech. Aside from the technical assistance I gained for coding problems, I also saw first-hand how excited people were to have me there. I had worried that as a 30-something new mum, people would laugh at me or see me as old and incapable of learning. Instead, I found people willing to help me become the best I could be and who would be open with me about my strengths (and weaknesses!) in a supportive environment. In large part, I have the Odin Project to thank for my success today.

Option 3: Paid Courses and Platforms

There's a running joke in the tech community that we all have multiple Coursera and Udemy courses sitting unused in our accounts. These platforms offer short courses, often (in my opinion, disingenuously) referred to as 'nano degrees'. These courses are delivered mainly via video and, as with any video course, their success or failure is mostly determined by the quality of the tutor.

Naturally, the best thing about these courses is that they are easily accessible, cheap (most courses range from $10 to $30), and relatively straightforward. You work through the programme and follow the teacher, and by the end, you should know something you didn't know before.

The downside, as I see it, is that there's nothing in these courses that ensures or enforces that you actually do any of the exercises or activities they set. As with YouTube, the temptation to just passively absorb information and say, 'Great! I know it now!' is still there in full force. Furthermore, even if you do the activities, there's nobody who will check them and give you active feedback. If you want that, you'll have to start exploring mentorship platforms or find someone online (or in your real life) willing to review your code.

As with any skill, having someone else review your code usually has a much bigger impact than reviewing your own code. Beginners aren't the best at knowing when they're doing something wrong or suboptimally. That's totally normal, of course, but does beg the question: 'How will I know if what I'm doing is good?' To my mind, the perfect course would involve some sort of active review from a real person, which in turn would enable you to move onto the next stage of learning.

Instead, what a lot of these courses offer is a view into 'ideal' solutions. These do give you a point of comparison, but again, who's going to tell you *why* the ideal solution is better? To me, this is where community and teamwork comes into play and why it's so crucial for those learning to code to have the opportunity to *talk about code as often as possible with real people*. I'll go into more detail on this later, but the basic idea is this: the two biggest tasks a professional developer has in their job is to write code and to talk about the code they and others write. If you develop the first skill and ignore the second, you're going to have a bad time and enter the job market woefully underprepared.

As of writing, there's one company, in particular, I want to shout out that offers a very good way around this. Although it's not perfect, Scrimba has developed a video platform with an inbuilt browser IDE. The instructors can break their courses down into small sections and have you complete exercises and run the code as if you were doing it on your own computer. Scrimba has also integrated comments as part of the platform so you can see what other students (and the tutor) have said with regard to each section of the course. For me, what makes this even better is that the company is extremely active on social media such as YouTube Live, allowing you to engage with other learners and with the tutors themselves.

Full disclosure: Scrimba has paid me to do interviews and podcasts with them in the past, so I'm not totally unbiased here. However, I learned React with their course by Bob Ziroll (who, since then, has become Scrimba's head of education) and fell in love with their system of learning long before they ever contacted me. It's a paid platform, but I don't get any 'cut' if you sign up there. I just think it's a great place to start transitioning from the fully web-based learning of freeCodeCamp and YouTube and start moving towards coding on your computer in an IDE. To me, it's the gateway drug into realistic software development for self-learners, so it would be remiss of me not to mention it here.

Option 4: Mentorship Communities

Mentorship communities are slowly growing in prominence. Personally, I haven't had a lot of experience with them, and right now, the industry is so fresh that it's hard to report back on how they work and what kind of results they can deliver.

In short, a mentorship community or mentorship platform enables experienced developers to be paired with junior developers or learners in order to organise 1-on-1 sessions where the mentor can act as a support. In general, these are not meant to be platforms for learning to code but rather for getting feedback on code or courses you're already completing.

Mentorship can be hugely beneficial. When I first began to code and found the Odin Project, I actually came roaring into their Discord server declaring that I needed one. I had some misconceptions about what a mentor is or should be that I'm guessing you, dear reader, may also have. So I want to take a moment to talk about what a mentor is and isn't.

- A mentor is not a teacher: A mentor will not bring you a course and a curriculum and say, 'Let's work through this material today.' The role of the mentor is not to teach you to code.

- A mentor can review code with you: A mentor can and should be willing to review the code you have written elsewhere. They may not set the assignment, but they can talk about it with you and point out any common pitfalls you might be falling into.

- A mentor is a guide: A mentor should also take an interest in your career and what you're looking for. Good mentors can help with code, great mentors can help with life.

- A mentor is not a cop: A mentor should not be policing what you do. Although they can recommend deadlines, the role is not one of authority and dictatorship but rather one of mutual understanding and learning.

This last point is the mistake I made; I thought that a mentor would help enforce my learning and make me stick to the promises I made myself. In the end, I didn't need a mentor, but I did end up finding a few developers who I felt particularly connected to and spoke to a lot while completing the Odin Project.

But let's get back to mentorship communities. Firstly, some are paid and some are free. Although we all love to jump at anything free, it's important to think carefully about what's more or less likely to happen in each system.

Although there are many wonderful developers out there willing to donate their time to a junior, in general, the ones who are more experienced, in high demand, or who are in high-paying jobs themselves will gravitate towards paid platforms as a way of managing risk. In other words, they don't want to waste their time on someone who's just stumbled onto a website and decided to give coding a try. They want juniors who are serious about their careers and their progress and are looking for real feedback on what they do. Charging a fee is a way of ensuring that.

Charging a fee also means that you as a learner are less likely to 'double-dip' and use multiple mentors. I strongly discourage you from attempting this. Every developer works a little bit differently, and many mentors will use certain 'mental models' to help you construct an understanding of code. By trying to use multiple mentors, you'll often find yourself receiving information which seems to conflict or which simply becomes confused because you're working with different people pushing different ideas of how to conceptualise code. Don't do it.

Most importantly, mentorship communities are not replacements for learning to code or any of the methods I've outlined previously. Any book on programming development would be remiss not to mention mentorship as an option, however it cannot and should not ever form the basis of your learning. If, however, you want to supplement a course and practice explaining and reviewing code with an actual person, it's a wonderful option.

Option 5: 'Bush Bashing'

'Bush bashing' is an Australian term. The bush is the Australian wilderness, thick, unruly, and often filled with dangerous terrain. Every year, tourists used to the wide, clear hiking paths of Europe or the USA find themselves needing a rescue crew in the Australian bush. Regardless, from time to time, we Australians enjoy 'bush bashing,' going off the track without any sort of path ahead of us. We 'bash' the bush because it's so impossible to walk through that we need to literally hit it away.

Similarly, when I've spoken to people about how they got started learning programming, this type of approach seems to arise: telling someone you can make something for them and then going for it. Much like bush bashing, there's no clear path for your learning, and the terrain is incredibly rocky. You might get lost and give up, and you might need rescuing. However, you might also find that, by bashing your way through, you learn a lot about the bush and come out the other side knowing the terrain pretty well.

Here are some examples:

- Make a website for a local business and give yourself a deadline
- Chat to a friend about some app they want to build and commit to building it together
- Find a friend who has a social media following and create their personal website

Simply put: bush bashing is not for the faint of heart.

If you're someone who's confident in your ability to learn quickly, responds well to pressure, and is ready to ask a LOT of questions online, then this could be a good option for you. Personally, I'd recommend doing self-learning for at least two to three months by yourself before attempting this. At least that way you can assess if you enjoy programming and you can get an idea of how to start.

The other downside of this approach is that, although you can build practical skills very well this way (by creating project after project), you're unlikely to learn the theoretical or conceptual side of programming very well or at all. Deadlines can be a great motivator, but they can also mean that you 'skip steps' in your learning, which could come back to bite you further down the track.

That said, many people have successfully gone from zero to successful careers using this option. Oftentimes, bush bashing goes hand-in-hand with a freelancing career, since your responsibility is to deliver results to the customer rather than to be the best at concepts, mentoring, or similar.

Overall, this is a hardcore method, but it is definitely a solid way to build practical skills if you can make it through.

What is 'Documentation' and How Do I Use It?

As soon as you begin learning any sort of programming, the word 'documentation' will begin rearing its head. Documentation is extremely important in programming and should always be your central source of information, much as a dictionary is a central source of information about a language. However, also like a dictionary, documentation often only shows part of the picture.

So what is documentation?

Documentation is a collection of information about a particular programming language, tool, or framework, which (in theory) explains what all the individual pieces of that system are. For example, one of the core pieces of online documentation for JavaScript is MDN Web Docs. MDN will allow you to look up any part of the language of JavaScript, for example Array.push(), and tell you what it is and how it works.

> ### Syntax
>
> ```
> push(element0)
> push(element0, element1)
> push(element0, element1, /* ... ,*/ elementN)
> ```
>
> ### Parameters
>
> **elementN**
> The element(s) to add to the end of the array.
>
> ### Return value
>
> The new `length` property of the object upon which the method was called.
>
> ### Description
>
> The `push` method appends values to an array.
>
> `push` is intentionally generic. This method can be used with `call()` or `apply()` on objects resembling arrays. The `push` method relies on a `length` property to determine where to start inserting the given values. If the `length` property cannot be converted into a number, the index used is 0. This includes the possibility of `length` being nonexistent, in which case `length` will also be created.
>
> Although strings are native, Array-like objects, they are not suitable in applications of this method, as strings are immutable. Similarly for the native, Array-like object arguments.

Every developer you meet will have strong opinions about documentation because, frankly, most of it's poorly written. MDN is an example of well-written documentation, but as a newcomer to programming, the above might as well be written in Greek. For me, as an experienced developer, I find it very clear and straightforward.

This is where the problem starts. Any developer with over a year of professional experience (sometimes less) will read documentation they think is clear and easy and send it to you to help you learn. You, however, do not yet have the foundational knowledge needed to truly understand what you're being sent. You'll read it. You'll be confused. You won't be any closer to solving your problem and, furthermore, you'll probably feel inadequate because a more experienced developer has told you how 'clear and straightforward' the documentation is.

Now that we've established why there'll be a mismatch between your teacher's reading of documentation vs your reading of documentation, let's look at what we can do about it.

Firstly, the above fact does not mean you should avoid reading documentation. Much as with any skill, the more you read it, the more it will start to make sense to you. You'll start learning the conventions that are used and your own internal 'programming dictionary' will expand. Once the terms 'property', 'values', 'native', 'generic', 'parameters', and 'method' are familiar to you, the sentences will fall into place. Part of how you learn this kind of terminology is, of course, by actively looking it up (we'll get to that), but part of it is just practice and familiarity, much as with any new vocabulary. So please, continue reading documentation, even when you feel overwhelmed after first reading it.

Secondly, this is the perfect time to apply my principle of using video platforms like YouTube as supplementary material to understand new terms. One of my first YouTube 'projects' was making short, three-minute videos explaining basic JavaScript concepts for exactly this reason.

Additionally, one thing developers love to do (and something I'll encourage you to do later!) is to write blog posts. A simple search (e.g. 'JavaScript array push explanation') should pull up articles in which you can read accounts from other beginners or teachers explaining the same concepts in simpler terms.

Here is how I would approach documentation for any given issue:

1. Read the documentation through once with a hot beverage of your choice. Don't take notes or try to understand it too deeply, just let it wash over you. Nevertheless, read every word.

2. Go to a video or blogging platform of your choice and look up two to three things explaining the same concept in simple language. This time, take the time to understand what's being said. Take notes.

3. Go back to the documentation and read it again *slowly*. Compare it to your notes and see how they describe it vs how you wrote it down.

Step 1 is about getting a basic familiarity with documentation and the ideas you need to learn about. Step 2 is about fostering a true understanding of the topic. Step 3 is about deepening your understanding of the concept and growing to better understand documentation language and structure.

If you approach documentation in this way, I guarantee you'll not only grow to understand and appreciate well-written documentation in the long-term, but, in the short-term, your understanding of any given programming concept will deepen and be far easier to recall.

Chapter 4

Creating a Learning Plan Using Agile Methodologies

In what probably feels like the distant future to you, you'll apply for tech jobs. Don't sweat about it now because this book will guide you through it. However, one thing you'll see again and again and again is 'agile methodologies'.

'Agile' is a buzzword in tech. The *physical* meaning of the word (being able to bend, be nimble, adapt quickly, etc.) more or less covers the work practice meaning as well. Agile as a concept is about creating small, realistic goals and working in short cycles to achieve them and release the results.

Before we begin, I should add that the below is written with self-learners in mind. If you're in a university program or a boot camp, you'll probably have more than enough content to keep you occupied. You could use the below to help you with any additional learning or out-of-course study you want to do.If, however, you're trying to learn alone or as part of an online community, this will be a good way for you to structure your time and you should read every word. Let's get started.

Introduction to Scrum

The most popular 'agile methodology' is scrum. For those who have an interest in rugby, I'm sorry to disappoint you by saying this has nothing to do with cramming together in a heap and...doing whatever happens in there with a ball. Rather, scrum is a system of teamwork and collaboration, which aims to use agile thinking to create great software quickly.

Let's quickly cover what's considered best practice in this area. At the start of a greenfield (new) project, an engineering team strives to create what's called an MVP (minimum viable product), which is the *absolute smallest version of a program* that could realistically be used. If this product was Twitter, for example, the MVP would involve logging in, posting something to your feed, viewing someone else's feed, and logging out. An MVP wouldn't have Twitter Spaces, Communities, chat groups, hashtags, retweets, etc.

Naturally, after the MVP is created, teams will have a list (the 'backlog') of features and fixes that are needed to continually improve the software. They'll work in short cycles (called 'sprints') of anywhere between a week and a month to complete a set of these tasks ('tickets'). These tickets will be given estimated difficulty levels and then selected for the sprint in 'planning', which is a meeting where you go through the currently prioritised tasks and decide what you can realistically achieve within the sprint time.

To continue the Twitter analogy, the next sprint might include the following tickets:

- As a user, I want to be able to follow other Twitter accounts so that I can see what my friends are saying.
- As a user, I want to be able to see tweets from accounts I follow so that I can stay up-to-date.

- As a user, I want to have a profile picture so that others can see what I look like.
- BUG: Usernames with the special character ~ throw an error.

That might be it! The engineering team would have one sprint to try to implement these features and fixes.

During the sprint, the team meets with each other every day for a 'daily standup' or daily. Traditionally, as the name suggests, this was done every day at the same time by all getting together in a room and standing up. In a daily, you go around the room and each person describes what they're working on, what problems they're facing, whether things are going well or not, and if there are any particular points they're stuck on or that they need help with. In this way, each team member regularly reflects on their own work and progress towards the sprint goal.

At the end of a sprint, teams usually undertake two events:

1. <u>The review</u>: The review allows the development team to meet with the product owner (the person representing the client or who decides priorities for product features) and outline what they completed and what they didn't complete.

2. <u>The retrospective</u>: Also known as a 'retro', this is for the development team to come together and talk about the sprint as a whole as well as to come up with ideas for how the next sprint could be better.

Once that's all done and dusted, whatever has been completed will be released. Tada! Twitter now has profile pictures, a 'Follow' button, and a news feed. Plus, I can make my username A~J~ROCKS without throwing any errors.

As you can imagine, the cycle now begins again: planning, dailies, review, release. These short release cycles and open communication (through dailies and retros) mean that the teams can stay agile. They can adapt to changes, re-prioritise things based on user feedback, and mix up the team structure if it's not working. Furthermore, the users are happy because they see new features and fixes coming in all the time!

Using Scrum as a Framework For a Learning Plan

There is a lot of terminology above which might make this process seem intimidating. Alternatively, you might be thinking that everything I've spoken about is a 'nice to know' for when you get your first job, but not necessary in the lead-up.

I want to challenge you to instead re-read the above with *learning goals* in mind. Let's take the enormous task of 'learning to programme' and break it down into tiny, manageable steps.

Selecting a Sprint Period

Time management is a skill of its own, and is not the topic of this book. However, I want you to think about the concept of 'agility' and what that might mean for managing your time. To me, it means selecting the *smallest possible amount of time* that you know for a fact you can commit to. Time management is always about priorities, so you need to sit down with your calendar and plan out exactly what your priorities are and where they'll fit.

For example, if you're working forty hours a week, have three kids, and do yoga three times a week, then perhaps programming ranks fourth in your list of priorities, and you can only commit to two hours of programming twice a week. Great! That's a start and is enough for you to slowly make progress. If, however, you recently got furloughed or graduated from school, are living with someone who's paying your bills, and have no kids, then perhaps you can more realistically commit to three hours a day, four days a week.

When it comes to any skill, the best way to learn is through consistent practice. What consistency looks like *to you* depends on your life circumstances. Of course, in an ideal world, we would all have six to eight hours a day, four to five days a week to learn to code. I'm guessing, though, that most people reading this are not in that kind of position. So take *the smallest possible amount you can commit to* and use that as the basis.

Before you read any further, revise your calendar, select those times, and *set a recurring schedule in your calendar*. If you're serious about learning programming, and I have to assume you are because you bought this book, then you should treat your sessions like immovable classes.

To select your sprint period, take that small amount of time and find how long it would take you to complete 20 hours of learning. The minimum amount is one week and the maximum is four weeks.

For Person A, two hours twice a week is four hours: $20 / 4 = 5$ weeks. Since we have a maximum of four weeks, that person would take four weeks.

For Person B, three hours a day for four days a week is twelve hours in a week: $20 / 12 = 1.6$. We'll round that up to two weeks.

Once you have your sprint period, you can move on to the next step.

Creating a Backlog

The next step is, of course, to create a backlog of what you need to get done. Remember, we are being *agile* here, so don't put pressure on yourself to get this perfectly right on the first try. Backlogs, like computer programs, need to change and adapt to your needs over time. What we're looking for here is to get a rough idea of the steps you have to take to achieve success.

Firstly, take a list of all the things you want to do (you can take them directly out of this book!) such as 'learn Git', 'learn HTML', 'learn CSS', etc.. Let's call them 'epics'. Then, start breaking those down into smaller tasks which we'll call 'stories': 'find an online course', 'download an IDE', 'watch Anna McDougall's video on HTML basics', and other completely non-self-promotional tasks.

You can use almost any medium to create this list. Some people like sticky notes, others use online whiteboards like Miro, to-do-list websites like Todoist or Trello, a simple text editor, or a spreadsheet app like Google Sheets or Excel. It really doesn't matter as long as you're able to find a way to move the tasks around as you need.

Here's an example of a starting backlog for someone wanting to learn web development:

- Learn to use an IDE
    - Look into the pros and cons of different IDEs
    - Choose an IDE
    - Install an IDE
    - Look into common plugins to add
    - Watch a video about how to use the IDE
- Learn HTML
    - Review freeCodeCamp and the Odin Project
    - Pick a learning platform
    - Complete the first chapter/unit of learning
    - Create a practice website based on the first unit
    - Watch a video about HTML basics and code along
- Learn Git
    - Read an introduction to Git
    - Create a GitHub profile
    - Learn three Git commands
    - Create a Git repository for a practice exercise

Estimation

The hardest part of any sprint is estimation, which involves trying to assign a difficulty level to each task. At the end of the sprint, you'll review how many 'points' of difficulty you got through (or didn't) so you can more accurately select tickets for the next sprint. Just to make things even more fun, the convention here is to use a Fibonacci sequence for estimating difficulty (1,2,3,5,8,13,21, etc.). For the sake of simplicity, I would encourage you to just use hours of time instead. It's not the 'Scrum way' but it'll keep things simpler and more concrete.

Naturally, that means you should go through your backlog and think about each task and how long you think it would take. Remember, we're staying *agile*. The goal is not to estimate everything precisely but rather to get a feeling for how you could fill the time you have. I would also recommend that you be conservative in your estimates. In other words, assume it'll take you longer than you think!

Let's have a look at our backlog again, this time with some estimates:

- Learn to use an IDE
    - Look into the pros and cons of different IDEs (1 hour)
    - Choose an IDE (0.5 hours)
    - Install an IDE (0.5 hours)
    - Look into common plugins to add (1 hour)
    - Watch a video about how to use the IDE and practice alongside (2 hours)

- Learn HTML
    - Review freeCodeCamp and the Odin Project (3 hours)
    - Pick a learning platform (0.5 hours)
    - Complete the first chapter/unit of learning (12 hours)
    - Create a practice website based on that first unit (10 hours)
    - Watch a video about HTML basics and code along (3 hours)

- Learn Git
    - Read an introduction to Git (2 hours)
    - Create a GitHub profile (1 hour)
    - Learn three Git commands (2 hours)
    - Create a Git repository for a practice exercise (2 hours)

Prioritise and Create your Sprint Backlog

Now comes the fun part. Go back to your sprint length estimates and see how many hours you'll be able to commit to a sprint *at a bare minimum*. If you remember Person A, they had four hours per week for four weeks, so their sprint would be sixteen hours. Person A's job would now be to look at all the tasks, prioritise them, and then pick out 16 hours (or fewer) worth of tasks to complete.

Don't delete or ignore the other tasks while undertaking this exercise. You'll need them for the next sprint and for 'extra tasks' to pick up if you achieve your sprint goal early.

Person A has finished and come up with her first sprint backlog:

1. Look into pros and cons of different IDEs (1 hour)
2. Choose an IDE (0.5 hours)
3. Install an IDE (0.5 hours)
4. Review freeCodeCamp and the Odin Project curricula (3 hours)
5. Pick a learning platform (0.5 hours)
6. Read an introduction to Git (2 hours)
7. Create a GitHub profile (1 hour)
8. Learn three Git commands (2 hours)
9. Create a Git repository for a practice exercise (2 hours)
10. Watch a video about HTML basics and code along (3 hours)

These 10 tasks are estimated to take 15.5 hours. Person A's first month of learning is now all planned out!

ANNA JEAN MCDOUGALL

During the Sprint

In this scenario, you don't have a team to check in with each day. Instead, you should be checking in with yourself any day you're programming. When I was learning, I did this via a journal.

Creating a journal of your learning is not only a great way to consolidate anything you've learned that day, but is also really lovely to look back on in future. I love reading my entries from when I was just starting to discover the wonder of programming! The entries don't have to be long, even just a few sentences will do, but they'll allow you to see, at a glance, what you were working on in your last session, any concepts you might want to look at again, etc.

The most popular way to track progress is on Twitter using the #100DaysOfCode hashtag. #100DaysOfCode is aimed at building habits by coding every day for 100 days straight. Although I think this is a very admirable goal, and thanks to online courses like freeCodeCamp it's also possible to do in very small chunks (meaning you could, for example, do five minutes every day), I nevertheless think it is unrealistic to ask you, dear reader, to commit to this. But feel free to use the hashtag. I'd also encourage you to use #CodeNewbies as well.

It might happen that you end up falling in love with programming and allocating much more time to it during the week than you had originally planned. Alternatively, you might find that you were *too* conservative with your estimates, and you're actually whipping through tasks far faster than expected. *No problem!* This is exactly why you have a backlog. If you complete your tickets ahead of the sprint end, you can simply pick up another one from the backlog and continue with that.

You might also find that some tasks end up being very similar to each other and can be combined or that you need to add extra tasks as you go because there were aspects of a topic you didn't realise existed. *No problem!* This approach is open to change. Alternatively, you might find that some tasks take twice as long as you thought. *No problem!* We're agile and open to failure. It's only by failing that we learn our limits. Take those lessons into your retrospective and your next sprint. Learn from them!

After the Sprint

Just as you will when you work as a developer, you should take at least an hour at the end of each sprint to sit down and evaluate how it went in your own, personal retrospective. If you have a mentor, this would be a great exercise to do with them.

Some questions you should ask yourself:

- Did I overestimate or underestimate how much time I would have?
- Did I overestimate or underestimate how long each task would take?
- Do I feel like I completed the tasks well and understood what I was doing?
- Am I closer to my end goal than I was before?
- Which strategies worked for me in this sprint? Which didn't?
- How could the next sprint be even better?
- Am I still motivated to continue learning?
- When I read back my first journal entry from this sprint, do I feel like I've progressed?

These questions will help you evaluate your learning.

I'm a huge fan of writing down the answers to these questions, and for that exercise, I recommend starting a blog. Blogging these answers not only allows you to reflect but provides some sense of outward accountability as well, especially if you're not working with a teacher, team, or mentor. If you're using social media while learning, you can post this blog post to Twitter or LinkedIn so that others can see your progress. They might even have recommendations for how you can improve for your next sprint!

After that, it's up to you if you want to dive straight back into planning the next sprint or if you want to take a day or two off between sprints to recover and/or consolidate your thoughts about your progress. Either way, congratulations! You've completed a sprint and are one step closer to creating a tech career for yourself!

Final Remarks on My 'Agile Learning' Approach

Goals and motivation are funny things. They wax, wane, and are often unpredictable. However, what we do know is that it's motivating to achieve goals and that feeling motivated leads you to create and work towards your goals. The two bounce off each other.

You'll notice that in the above approach, I continually advise you to make things easier for yourself by:

- Planning around the minimum amount of time you can dedicate, not the maximum
- Estimating more time than you think you'll need for tasks
- Breaking tasks down into smaller and smaller steps
- Allowing yourself a bit of time off between sprints

These pieces of advice are not just 'busy work'. They're designed to give you small, achievable goals to cross off your list. Setting your schedule based around your minimum means that anything extra is a bonus, and if you're feeling particularly motivated some weeks, you *can and should* allow yourself to dive in headfirst and do more than you expected.

If you planned to program two days per week but found you could actually manage three days, how would you feel? If, on the flip side, you committed yourself to programming every day of the week, but found you only had three days you could reliably set aside, how would you feel? The end result is the same, the difference lies in your feelings of pride and success.

You're starting to learn a new thing that has a lot of facets and takes a lot of time to master. Be kind to yourself. Be realistic in what you can do.

If you have days where you sit at the computer and find yourself feeling deflated, try to learn for just ten minutes. If, after those ten minutes, you still feel like watching *Star Trek* and eating popcorn, then go watch *Star Trek* and eat popcorn. No shame. No guilt. We all need time off sometimes! All I want you to promise me is that you'll do those ten minutes at the times you plan to do them.

Furthermore, I really want to know how this plan works for you and what tools you use to bring your learning to life. Get in touch and, if you're willing, please share your templates with me so I can pass them on to the rest of the community.

Chapter 5

Non-Programming Jobs

The focus of this book is on building programmers: web developers, app developers, software engineers, and more. I believe that everyone can learn to code. As with any skill, some people will pick it up easily and it will feel 'natural' to them. For most people, however, it won't.

Regardless of which group you fall into, consistent practice and a dedication to learning are essential. With this kind of effort, the 'average' person will become a better programmer than the natural talent who slacks off because they're bored or unmotivated. If you're lucky enough to have both talent and drive, then you'll make this a career more easily than most. However, of those two factors, drive is the only one I would deem *essential*.

With that said, you can absolutely become a programmer, and by applying this section's teachings meaningfully and seriously to your life, you'll get there. So, please don't doubt that you *can* become a programmer, but there might come a time when you realise that programming is not what you *want*.

I have no doubt that if I dedicated time and effort to it, I could be a great swimmer for my age. I have long limbs and strong legs, and if I went to the pool every day and followed a good progressive programme that challenged me within my abilities, I would probably do a great job at it within a few years. However, I only enjoy swimming for fun. I go rarely, and when I do it's usually more to relax and enjoy the water than it is to get good lap times or improve my stroke. In short, I don't *want* to apply the effort needed to be a great swimmer. Swimming doesn't fire me up. Swimming isn't what I want to pursue. It isn't a priority for me.

Similarly, after you've been learning to code, you may find that you *can* do it. You may even find that you're a natural at it! However, the chance still remains that you realise it doesn't fire you up. You're interested, but it isn't a priority for you. There's no shame in this, and there are plenty of other ways to get involved in tech that bring a lot of value to the industry.

Don't get sucked into the mindset that programming is the only skill that matters. As you'll see in later chapters, the technical side is only the beginning, even if you do decide to become a developer.

So, let's quickly look at five jobs in tech you could pursue that are less programming-heavy but still central to tech. Having any sort of experience in programming gives you an advantage in these positions but is usually not a requirement.

Product Owner

Product owners are probably the main topic of complaint for professional developers, but don't let that deter you. These are the people who get to make the major decisions regarding the direction of the software. If you find that you often have strong opinions on what an app should do, how it should look, and how it should respond to users, then this (or UI/UX design) could be a great option for you.

Imagine a company hires a software consultancy to build a mobile app that helps manage their brand of smart toasters. The company, Toaster Inc., is the one paying the bills. They know toasters better than anyone, but they don't understand software or the development process. They might have a good idea of what they want out of an app as an end user, but the technical implementation of that application is something they know little to nothing about.

Toaster Inc. might choose someone, potentially a marketing manager or similar, to represent their company and advocate for what the app should do. In such a scenario, the marketing manager usually finds that, although they know what Toaster Inc. wants, they don't know how to answer the questions the development team asks them. It could be in this environment that a professional product owner is hired: someone who is familiar with the basics of application development but who mostly acts as an advocate for Toaster Inc. In Scrum, a product owner has to attend a lot of the same meetings as developers but makes broader decisions about the priorities for the application.

For example, after discussing it with the developers, it may become clear that only one of the five separate but similarly desired features can be implemented this month. Which feature should it be? What do the smart toaster users (or Toaster Inc.) want to be able to do with their app? This is the kind of decision a product owner makes.

Scrum Masters and Project Managers

If you're unfamiliar with Scrum, you won't realise how heretical it is for me to mention these two jobs in the same header. Come back to this book in a few years and curse me then!

Both of these roles have to do with liaising, or balancing the needs of the product owner(s) with the needs of developers. In short, they involve overseeing the processes and systems in place to ensure the work gets done effectively.

In the case of a Scrum Master, this goal is achieved by adhering to the Scrum guidelines, keeping everyone apprised of changes in a way that is open and communicative, and in many ways helping to motivate and drive progress by facilitating good practices in a team. In short, you would want to be a 'people person' for this role.

Project managers should, officially speaking, not exist in Scrum teams. However, the job title is often used liberally and, in many cases, a project manager will act as a half-Scrum Master, half-budgeter/project lead. This often involves working with timelines and spreadsheets and keeping on top of how things are progressing. The main difference between the two jobs is that the project manager tends to be seen as 'responsible' for the project, whereas the Scrum Master tends to be viewed as 'facilitating' the project.

Both of these jobs are made much easier if you yourself have worked as a developer at some point. Most of these positions are filled by ex-developers. However, it's certainly not a requirement and, as many developers tend not to be people-driven, having that on your side is a distinct advantage.

If you're interested in developing these skills, I recommend looking into the official Scrum Master training and certification (visit www.scrum.org or search for PSM - Professional Scrum Master courses in your area). Even if you're more interested in project management, most development teams use some form of agile practices, so getting a foundational understanding and certification in Scrum will also help you get hired. Try to gain experience by working with others training to be developers, finding a mentor who already works as a scrum master, or finding a friendly startup who is willing to let you sit in on meetings for a week or a month so you can see what it's like in practice. This will help offset the lack of experience you'll have in professional development environments.

ANNA JEAN MCDOUGALL

UI/UX Designers

This job truly straddles the line between development and design. A basic understanding of front-end programming (e.g. HTML, CSS, and perhaps a CSS framework like Bootstrap, Tailwind, or Material UI) is extremely helpful here. However, the broad majority of the work is not programming.

UI stands for 'user interface' and UX stands for 'user experience'. User interface is the what and how of any application: what colours are used, where are the buttons, how are the components laid out, where is the header/footer/navigation bar, etc. User experience focuses on what a user wants, enjoys, or dislikes about using a website. For example, a common tenet of user experience is to 'minimise clicks' to get a user where they most commonly want to go.

User experience is (or rather, should be) the basis for any user interface. For example, if you're designing a user interface for our Toaster Inc. app and it takes ten clicks (or finger touches) to rename your custom smart toaster, then you're providing a bad user experience because it takes the user too long to complete a common task.

The role of the UI/UX designer is, therefore, to think deeply about what a user wants to experience, combine that with what features are (planned to be) available, and then design wireframes to represent the different sections of a website or application. These designs form a basis for the front-end developers to use when creating the app.

The downside with UI/UX is that not every company uses specialists of this kind, so the demand is not as high as it is for more technical- or business-based roles. However, there's a growing awareness of the importance of using specialists in this field, especially as the breadth of services being offered through such applications increases.

As a small aside: This is actually what I originally thought I would be!

Tech Recruiters

The tech job market is HOT. It's so hot that the field isn't just expanding for engineers, but also for those who hire them. If you find that you're good with people and enjoy talking to engineers more than *being* an engineer, then this could be the career for you.

A recruiter with some actual technical understanding is highly sought after. Very often, you see recruiters from other industries transitioning horizontally into technical recruitment. They have no idea what technical terminology means, what different technologies do, etc. A once-viral tweet joked that tech recruiters would message you asking if you know how to 'connect to a database using CSS', with CSS being a system which controls colours and positioning and has nothing to do with data storage.

In short, if you can make decent progress learning programming, are good with people, and are willing to work hard to form long-term relationships with engineers, then you can make a good career for yourself in this role.

Of those things, forming long-term relationships is the most crucial. As a recruiter, your day-to-day work will involve finding and interviewing new potential candidates. However, your career's success will be built on the backs of solid relationships, not only with people and companies you work with but those with whom it doesn't work out as well.

For example, many companies are seeking senior talent. You might find that multiple candidates you recommend get turned away for lack of experience. Rather than throwing their files out or ghosting them, part of your job will be to keep open lines of communication with them. Why? Because in a few years they *will* be senior talent.

If this is an area of interest for you, I highly recommend connecting with Taylor Desseyn on LinkedIn. He's a solid acquaintance and a great example of technical recruiting done right. His website (*Recruiter Against Recruiters*) provides terrific resources for engineers and jobseekers and, at the time of writing, he's also doing regular live sessions on LinkedIn where he discusses the field of technical recruiting in general.

Developer Advocates

Developer advocates (also known as "dev advocates" or "avocadoes" as a long-running joke) are a relatively new job in the world of tech, and they represent a blend between technical skills, marketing, and customer service skills. Usually they work for a product or company which targets developers as their main customer or user. For example, Amazon Web Services (AWS) is one of the leading cloud service providers, and most of those using their services are developers or technical leads. Although they have people who can provide help in emergencies, or with technical problems, the role of a developer advocate goes beyond this.

The developer advocate has to understand both their product and the developers using them: they understand the technical challenges being faced, and are great communicators about why a certain product is useful, what niche it fills, and how to best leverage it.

Dev advocates often act as the public face of a product and talk about it a lot on social media. Many of them also specialise in producing some type of content for the product or the typical situations/languages in which that product is used. For example by writing blog posts, creating YouTube tutorials, or even being charged with writing the documentation itself.

If you've found that you love coding and programming, but also love the networking and communication aspect, then this could be a great choice. The job itself often doesn't involve programming, and programming skill is *usually* a secondary requirement for these jobs. In other words, you need to be able to understand code, but you don't need to be the most amazing programmer.

What you do need is the ability to drill down into one niche product or topic, and love communicating about that same topic. Rather than being an expert on programming, you become an expert on what problems your product can solve. Ideally, you should already have some experience with writing, blogging, video creation, radio, conferences/networking, or similar.

One quick proviso: if you want to continue programming as part of your job, even as just a small part, it is important to mention this when interviewing. I've heard plenty of stories of developer advocates who think they'll still get to code but end up not touching an IDE in months. That might be exactly what you're looking for, but if it isn't then it's important you speak up for yourself during the interview process.

Key Takeaways

Tech is an enormous field. You don't know how enormous it is. I don't know how enormous it is. It is for this reason that it's important not to try to understand everything but rather to pick a set of skills and tools which are commonly paired together and then to learn those. As you learn more, you'll start to come into contact with other areas of tech, and slowly but surely you'll find your niche. Perhaps that niche doesn't even involve programming.

What's most important at this stage is that you be realistic. What can you handle? How much time can you commit to this that will keep you progressing but motivated? What level of priority will you give learning this skill when compared to other parts of your life?

All of these things combined will help you form a plan. But that plan does not have to be finalised now.

One of the most important concepts throughout the tech industry is *agility*. Although you don't work in tech yet, by learning these concepts early and applying them to how you work now, you'll already be at an advantage when it comes to interviewing and fulfilling your work duties later.

Having an agile mindset isn't just about working in sprints and setting small goals, it's also about being ready for failure and using that failure as a jumping-off point for change.

In this section, you've learned not only some of the essential skills you must learn but also how you can learn them given the restrictions and priorities you have. Furthermore, you've learned about the mental obstacles you're likely to face as you work towards some form of basic mastery: facing the depths of despair as you hit the Dunning-Kruger effect and confronting your own ignorance and weaknesses with imposter syndrome. With our lesson on recall vs recognition, you've hopefully grown to understand why watching YouTube videos will never be as effective as getting your fingers on the keyboard and trying to work something out on your own. Lastly, you've learned about five different, in-demand jobs in the tech industry that don't involve programming. They're not there to unmotivate you. Learning programming will be a huge advantage in any of those fields. However, they do show you that if you don't become a developer, hope is not lost. There are other skills you can improve and other ways you can be part of the future.

As I mentioned at this section's opening: you're a risk to companies. Learning technical skills is the bare minimum you need to begin applying to jobs. By learning them alongside skills like version control, understanding documentation, and adopting an agile mindset, you'll be in a position to provide concrete examples in job interviews of what makes you uniquely qualified to take on a role. Each one of these skills is one less risk your potential employer has to take.

There are also other technical skills that I'll tackle in Section 3, namely data structures and algorithms. You'll come across these naturally as you learn your chosen programming language, but I'll give you some more guidance with regard to training when we get to interview requirements. Suffice it to say: it isn't as scary as it sounds.

Building technical skills is essential to the job search, but it's usually insufficient without support from outside. Where this support comes from, and how you can find it, is what our next section will cover.

Section 2
Who You Are

Finding Your Identity and Growing A Community

Many people attracted to technical careers tend to be the type who don't enjoy promoting themselves. A common phrase you'll hear among techies is that they want to 'let the work speak for itself.' Therefore, many people learn the skills, create great projects, put them online, and then sit back and wait for Google or Netflix to call them. Unfortunately, that's just not how it works.

In order for your work to speak, somebody needs to be listening, and nobody will be listening if they aren't interested in *you*. So, how do you get your technical skills noticed, especially when you're the kind of candidate whose CV isn't littered with the work experience, degrees, and keywords that recruiters love? The answer is twofold: a network and a community.

For the most part, I'll use the terms 'network' and 'community' interchangeably, but in general, you can think of a network as being 'people you know' and a community as being 'the group you belong to'. The lines become blurred once you start venturing into the world of social media, where a seemingly random group of people (a network) can become more closely connected over time and end up forming communities.

I mention time here because it's a crucial factor. **Let me state it simply: if you start networking on the first day of your job search, you're too late**. It takes time to get to know people in tech, form a reputation, or learn about the scene in your chosen field. Furthermore, you never know when one of your connections might recommend you for a job or forward an opportunity to your inbox.

The sooner you start building your online presence, the easier it will be to apply to jobs with 'social proof' of your dedication to tech. By that I mean not only the people who can vouch that you're the real deal but also online content, such as blog posts, that you can point an employer to and say, 'Look! Here! See how much I want to do this and how well I can explain it to others! Wouldn't I be a great colleague?' We'll come back to 'social proof' over and over again in this section because it's the cornerstone of what we're trying to achieve here.

Furthermore, a lot of the documents and best practices we'll cover in Section 3 will be based upon the exercises and activities you do in this section. Jumping into the job search becomes significantly easier when you already know who you are, what you have to offer beyond code, who to ask to give you tips for an upcoming interview, and what examples you should use to show that you're not a risky hire.

There's one more massive benefit to networking, which cannot be overstated: networking helps your technical skills. Here is an incomplete list of the skills you can develop by being part of a programming community:

- Reading other people's code
- Explaining your coding decisions
- Pair programming (solving a coding problem together)

- Learning to take criticism without taking offence
- Giving appropriate feedback to others
- Optimising code beyond being just functional

All of the above makes you a better programmer and (eventually) a better team member. Luckily for you, they'll also help you land a job.

I mentioned in the introduction of this book that Twitter is how I landed my job as a junior software engineer. By tweeting about my programming journey and helping others with theirs through blog posts and YouTube videos, I gained a solid following on Twitter. When the time came for me to find my first programming job, I created a video cover letter in which I explained who I was, the experience I had outside of tech, what I was looking for, and why I was so sure I could handle it. That tweet got me over a dozen job leads in my inbox in under 24 hours. Ten days later, I was hired without even having to complete a technical interview.

Networking is just as important for a junior as building technical talent because a significant proportion of juniors are hired on belief in their potential rather than existing expertise. The video, my tweets, my blog posts, and my YouTube videos didn't prove I was an amazing programmer, but they did prove that I was a good communicator about programming concepts, that I was excited to learn, and that I was someone other people liked to be around. Since I had the technical skills, I would have been hired eventually by slowly but surely sending off CVs and cover letters and plugging away at technical interviews. But because I had the social proof, I got hired before my certification was completed and with a higher starting salary than anyone else in the history of my course provider.

I say all this not to brag but purely to show how big of an impact this section can have if you take it seriously. In general, my goal is to have you end up in the same position, where people approach you to ask if you're looking for work rather than for you to have to apply to hundreds of jobs and wait years for someone to believe in you. Remember, this process is about proving you're not a risk to hiring managers. The more proof you can provide, the better.

Aside from all of those pragmatic and logical benefits, there is one more major advantage to growing a community: learning is more fun when you have others alongside you—people to talk to, people to learn about, people to vent to, and people to ask questions when you get stuck.

Transitioning into a new field is *hard*, and doing it alone is scary. Working with others makes riding the highs and lows of the Dunning-Kruger Effect a little less frustrating and a little more fun!

Chapter 6

Creating a Brand Identity and Using the Tricks of the Trade

I hate the idea of marketing people in the same way we market products. Humans are not the same as vacuum cleaners, the latest iPhone, or a new cereal. Branding, USPs, elevator pitches—all of these things can feel dehumanising. Using these tactics just so people remember us, call us, hire us, and reference us can leave us feeling like they only know a small part of who we are, rather than the complex whole.

Unfortunately, they work.

Like it or not, there are a few facts about the human brain that make strangers less than receptive to whole and complex truths about other people. For example, brains love searching for and 'discovering' patterns, even when those patterns aren't related to the truth. For example, when I was a little kid, I was convinced that winking at the traffic lights would make them turn green faster because that was the coincidence I observed over and over again. This unfortunate habit also tends to lead to prejudice and discrimination, whether conscious or subconscious, as people project the patterns they see and hear onto the people around them.

Another fact about the brain and memory is that the more distinct or weird something is, the more likely you are to remember it. Why? Because it breaks the expectations we have formed using this tendency to search for patterns. Once something falls outside a pattern or an expectation, it becomes 'memory-worthy'. For example, memory champions (yes, they're a thing) have a trick for remembering names and faces: find the most distinctive feature about someone you meet (eg long earlobes), then pair it with some sort of word association for their name (eg Jonas becomes "john' and 'ass') and imagine a situation where these things interact (eg, someone sitting on the 'john' (toilet) and having their long earlobes touch their ass). This sounds *super weird* and that's because it is; the weirder these connections, the more likely you are to be able to remember them later.

Similarly, we want to use some basic tenets of marketing and sales to create a profile that's *uniquely you*. We want you to be weird enough to remember while also presenting your story confidently and without any hesitation. I don't love using these tactics for human beings; by purposefully boiling you down into your essence, we'll lose some of your complexity. However, at least we have total control over this narrative and the features we focus on. The fact that you're probably *not* someone who neatly fits into the tech-bro box means that we can also be proud of that fact and use it as one of the points that can help people remember you.

Is it a perfect way forward? No. But knowing some branding basics will help you form profiles on social media, in communities, and your job application documents later.

Having sales tools in your kit, applying them to yourself as 'the product', and being consistent in their usage will get you much further than trying to explain the breadth and depth of your life, soul, and personality to every person you meet. There's plenty of time to dive deep when you have more extensive conversations in future, but what we're concerned with here is getting people to the point where they want to have extensive conversations with you at all. This applies to online communities, job applications, new friends, and even potential romantic relationships. Despite my philosophical objections, these tools tend to increase how well people want to know you.

Let's go to the dark side together and learn how to use them effectively so you can start your career in tech more easily.

Branding and the Three-Words Approach

Branding is probably a word you associate with major trademarked corporations, but the truth is that branding is a core part of almost every business out there. Branding is the idea of distilling the essence of who you are and what you offer down into some easily comprehensible concepts.

In marketing, branding is usually related to things like logos, catchphrases, advertising jingles, and colour schemes. For example, a company selling skateboards to teenagers probably wouldn't get far with pastel colours and relaxing imagery. Rather, their brand would likely be packed with intense colours, perhaps paired with black, and built around words like 'rebellious', 'energetic', and 'daring'.

In corporate communications, branding is also often used as part of the value proposition for potential employees. In my first job as a software engineer, my employer deemed brand words as 'values', including 'goal-oriented', 'thrilled', and 'humourous', which made me feel at home as someone who identifies with all of those emotions. If they had had the words 'traditional', 'detail-oriented', and 'serious' as their value words, I might have thought twice about working there.

For individuals, branding is about trying to find the core of who you are and what you offer. A great way to learn about branding is to step into the world of Instagram. Start searching for accounts on any topic you have an interest in, and you'll quickly find big-name influencers who consistently use the same colours, fonts, and styles for all their posts. Some even have specific outfits or props that they use. The goal here isn't to portray the wide range of interests they (probably) have in the real world but rather to target one specific audience who is interested in one specific thing. By having something unique that identifies them (eg a prop, colour, funny name, font, etc) they create a trigger for you to remember them by. By consistently using that thing, they are able to breed a sense of familiarity and trust. After a while, you immediately recognise that person and their content and are inclined to read and trust it. This is the goal of branding.

Naturally, you can go as deep as you want into the world of branding. I'll use a lot of the above ideas to help you craft your social media for networking and searching for a job later in this section. For now, though, let's focus on just one simple exercise: the three-words technique.

Get a piece of paper and a pen or open a new document on your computer and complete the following. Try your best not to read ahead for each step:

1. Spend two minutes writing down every adjective that you could use to describe yourself. Don't put a limit on how many you write. Anything is viable. These words should fill in the blank of 'I am a ____ person.' (eg 'funny', 'pessimistic', 'dog-loving', 'open-minded', 'helpful', 'hungry', 'overeducated', 'very tall', 'aggressive', etc).

2. If you're lucky enough to have coworkers, housemates, or family members who you like, ask them how they would describe you in three to five words. Add any that weren't on your list.

3. Delete or strike out any words that an employer would immediately dismiss (eg 'pessimistic' and 'aggressive').

4. Delete any words that you feel don't *quite* capture you completely. (eg 'hungry', 'overeducated').

5. With the words you have left, pick two that are quintessentially you and that you can imagine employers really looking for (eg 'open-minded', 'helpful').

6. Lastly, pick one that still fully captures you, but which is maybe a little quirkier (eg 'dog-loving', 'very tall', or even bring back 'hungry'!).

7. Congratulations! You have your three words!

The three words you have chosen should encapsulate who you are, not *all* of who you are (because obviously that's not possible in just three words) but the core of what you will present to the outside world. The first two words will be your value proposition to employers and your network, and the last word is the 'memory trigger', the thing that makes people smile and that you can use to keep reminding them of who you are.

These three words will be used over and over again in the coming chapters and in your job application, so get very comfortable with them. You should love them, and they should feel comfortable and accurate. If your 'quirky word' isn't something you want to talk about or reference repeatedly, go back and choose a different one. Repetition is part of our branding strategy, so it's important that you only select words here that you're happy to repeat in reference to yourself time and again.

For me, the words I landed on were 'energetic', 'helpful', and 'quirky'. My high energy brings a lot of value to teams, as it often helps energise others as well. My helpfulness means I'm willing to lend a hand and do more than just what's required. And although I wouldn't have personally chosen 'quirky' for myself, it was a word that came up time and again with my friends, and my odd 'theatre-kid' energy is something that does make me memorable, so I decided to embrace the weirdness! Will being quirky get me a job? Unlikely. However, by having this word as part of my brand, it humanises what would otherwise be just a list of buzzwords.

Unique Selling Point

Along similar branding lines as the three-words technique, but with a very different focus, is the unique selling point, commonly known in the sales and marketing world as a USP. Just as the name suggests, the idea of a USP is to boil down what you have to offer and find what makes you different while still adding value. In other words, it's the answer to the question, 'What can you bring to this position that other candidates won't?'

This question can seem incredibly daunting if you don't, in fact, feel like you have anything special to offer. Perhaps you see yourself as just an average Jane wanting a new career with nothing special to offer. I already know that's not true because you're reading this book and taking the initiative in planning out your next steps. That shows drive and a willingness to put in the work, which already puts you ahead of most people. If you're able to carry out this book's recommendations, you will have also proven yourself to be highly motivated, organised, and consistent in learning, which, in my opinion, already puts you in the top 10% of candidates.

However, I'm also willing to bet that there's something else. Something you're interested in or passionate about that other people find hard to understand. Alternatively, perhaps you have a career under your belt already that you were relatively successful in. A third option is that you have been through some sort of medical ordeal, or taken care of someone who has, and have had to show perseverance to get through that rough patch.

There are many different sources you can pull from regarding your USP, and perhaps you're lucky enough to already know what it's going to be. For me, it was my former career as an opera singer. If you're unsure what yours could be, try the following steps:

1. Think about your three brand words and add each one as a heading to a new document or sheet of paper.

2. Try to dive into each adjective and ask the question, 'What event(s) in my life have made me that way?' Write down any and all answers that occur to you, including jobs, pets, relationships, health, family, etc.

3. Pick three that you feel have had the biggest impact on your life and/or personality.

4. For each of these three, try to write out three ways that event has made you a better person. (eg 'Breaking my leg at the height of my hockey career made me learn to handle negative emotions and use them constructively').

5. Now, try them on for size: write out the phrase, 'I'm a software engineer and _____' for each one (eg, 'I'm a software engineer and former hockey player, 'I'm a software engineer and cancer survivor', 'I'm a software engineer and former contestant on *The Bachelor*', etc).

6. For this next part, you need an empty living space or a soundproof room. Have a conversation with yourself that's like a mock interview. Introduce yourself with the phrase you wrote down in point five, explain why you're suitable for the job and what skills the event gave you (via your notes from point four), and then wrap up with '...and that's why I'm uniquely qualified to take on the challenges of this role.'

By the end of this activity, you'll hopefully know which of the phrases feels the strongest. If there are still multiple contenders, *outsource it!* Go to your network or your mentor or talk to a friend or trusted family member and explain what you're trying to do. There may be different opinions, but there is often one clear winner, and an outside perspective will help you find it. The goal of the exercise is to find something that has a strong tie-in with being a good employee while also making you memorable.

Again, your USP will become a core part of everything you do during and in the lead-up to your job search, so become very comfortable with it!

The Elevator Pitch

If you've never heard of an elevator pitch, then allow me to provide you with some mental imagery. Let's say you've always wanted to work for Meta (formerly Facebook), and one day on your way to a dentist's appointment, you hop in an elevator going to the tenth floor. As you enter the elevator, you're shocked to see Sheryl Sandberg (chief operating officer of Meta) standing in front of you. You now have less than a minute to convince her to hire you.

This thought experiment has been used in many different sales contexts over the years. The person in the elevator changes and the goal of the talk changes (eg sell a product, invest in a new business, etc), but the idea is the same: distil what you have to offer into a small, catchy package that makes someone not only remember you but *want* to call you.

So, how do you construct an effective elevator pitch? You guessed it! I'm going to recommend using a combination of your three words and your USP.

In the final step of the USP exercise, I asked you to talk to yourself about how your USP makes you a better employee. When you did this exercise, you most likely found that you spoke longer than expected. It can sometimes take a while to truly explain the connections between an event and an engineering career. In my 2021 conference presentation "Being an Opera Singer Prepared me for a Programming Career" (also available on YouTube), it took me seven minutes. That's far too long for an elevator pitch!

Instead, you need to take *only one* of your USP arguments and combine it with your three words. For example, one of my USP arguments is that being an opera singer made me totally comfortable on stage, meaning that I'm someone who's always happy to hold workshops and share my knowledge with other developers both internally and externally.

There are many different ways to approach an elevator pitch, and there are many books and blog posts that can help guide you to incredible and creative options. However, here's an example of just one way you can craft it:

1. A short introduction to yourself using your USP immediately
2. Your one-sentence connection between your USP and the job you want
3. An offer to reduce a pain point for the other person (ie solve one of their problems) using two to three of your key adjectives

Here's my attempt:

> 'Hi, I'm Anna McDougall. I'm a software engineer who used to be an opera singer. You might think those things sound completely different, but being a former singer gives me a superpower in technical circles since I'm comfortable in front of a crowd and always happy to present at conferences and share my knowledge. If your dev teams ever need an energetic, helpful person to help lift them up technically and personally, you can call me. Here's my card.'

This isn't something that will feel natural or normal to you *at all*, and that's OK. Remember that, for most of your life, you've probably been taught to be humble and not to brag. You have to resist the urge to litter your pitch with 'just', 'only', 'kinda', 'like', 'I think', 'hopefully', and other words that diminish the strength of it. It should still sound like you but the *most confident* you.

Once you're happy with your elevator pitch (and that could take hours, days, or weeks to achieve) it's essential that you practice it until you can memorise it, then practice it until it feels like normal conversation. Write it on a Post-it or stick it above your desk and recite it once or twice a day.

You can use this pitch later when in job interviews but also adapt it for meetups, social media profiles, and more. This is a great piece of speech to have up your sleeve, and if you practice it enough, then it will feel and sound totally natural, no matter how awkward it feels now. Eventually, you'll also get to the point of being able to change the wording on-cue to adapt to your audience.

Chapter 7

Social Media Profiles: Dos and Don'ts

Having the Chapter 6 tools under your belt and ready to go will help you a lot when creating social media profiles. In this chapter, we'll explore how to translate these tools into an effective profile for use online. As someone who has worked for many years in digital marketing, I have a lot of opinions on this. However, as this is a book focused specifically on career transitions, I'll keep this section as direct as possible. Suffice it to say that I have more tips and information about these topics available online, and if you really want to dive deep into this topic, my YouTube channel is more than happy to oblige!

Before we begin, it's important to note that, although having the same colours and fonts in your profile isn't *essential*, it's helpful for creating consistent, recognisable content. Canva is one of the easiest places to create a 'brand kit' for any images or posts you use on social media. Alternatively, you can also sit down with your favourite Paint-like programme and try out your name in a bunch of fonts until you find one you like paired with colours that match the words you chose in Chapter 6. Try to use these colours and fonts wherever possible in visual material.

Another important thing to note is that if you're not interested in your social media profiles becoming tech-heavy and use them a lot for personal contacts, pizza reviews, or cake decoration tips, then it's worth considering creating a new profile specifically for this purpose. The downside is that you'll have to build it up from nothing, but the upside is that you'll be able to craft an amazing profile from the beginning. Of course, you don't need to post *solely* about tech from now on, but the idea is to create *social proof* that you're a low-risk choice for employers. If they can see that you regularly post about tech, have a lot of followers also interested in tech, and are well-respected in tech spaces, then it's harder for them to see you as a risky newbie to the industry. In other words, you're creating the impression that you're *already* in the industry. Employers nowadays are almost certain to search for you on social media, so having this kind of proof available and filed under your real name is extremely valuable down the road.

That said, let's jump straight into some of the things most social media platforms have in common, the mistakes I see over and over again, and how to do them right.

Cover Image

A cover image is a banner-like image that is displayed across the top of your profile, nestled behind your profile photo. It's a wonderful thing to have because it enables you to set the tone of your profile before anyone has even read your name.

There are a variety of ways you can utilise this real estate to best promote yourself and your abilities based on what your branding is like. For example, tech Twitter celebrity Danny Thompson has always focused on his community work, and so, his cover images usually include pictures of him working with beginner developers in workshops, in a group photo from an event, or standing on a stage to speak.

Since I got into tech in COVID times, I didn't have these kinds of photos to work with, so I used a banner with my three words emblazoned across it in my brand colours and font instead. If you watch some of my older YouTube videos, you'll still see my intro includes the same words and colours. Nowadays, since I'm no longer searching for a job, my profile is based on the title of this book: *You Belong in Tech*. I've also used "Getting You into Tech".

If, like me, you decide to use words, try to keep it short and direct. Quotes are fine, but not essays. If you do use a quote, try to keep it related to the job you want or your attitude toward work or learning. Imagine the quote being posted above your desk at a cubicle in the office.

Yet another option is to have a great photo of your local area, such as a silhouette of your city skyline. This is a good option if you're looking for a job local to you rather than remote or international.

On some social media platforms, like Twitter, the 'Follow' button is directly beneath your cover image. This provides the opportunity to use arrows to encourage people to follow you. A common one is 'Hi! I'm [name] and I tweet about ___. Follow me!' paired with the arrow. This is also a great, direct way to have people know what you're about quickly, and it comes with another classic marketing concept: the *call to action*.

A call to action (CTA) is basically a request to do something, the classics being 'Click here!', 'Read more', and 'Visit.' We'll come back to these soon because calls to action can be very effective when you know exactly what you want to achieve in your profile.

Profile Picture

Your profile picture appears everywhere on your social media platforms. It's the picture people are most likely to recognise you by, and it's probably *the* thing you must get right.

The ideal profile picture is a photo of you smiling at the camera in good light. That's it. That's my big rule.

Despite this seemingly simple guideline, plenty of people try to do other things with their profile pictures, and nine times out of ten, it doesn't land the way they think it will. Common mistakes include not looking at the camera, dark or blurry shots, clashing colours (eg a blue shirt on a blue background), intense stares, and shots that are too far away to reasonably recognise the person.

If you can afford to, it's always worth having a professional photographer take some headshots. Ideally, you could come away with three to four photos you really love, but really, you only need one absolute winner. If you can't afford a photographer, get a friend or family member to go with you to a local park or garden with a lovely green background (or a background of tree bark, which somehow always looks good), and take the photos with their phone about an hour before sunset. That's the 'golden hour' of lighting for photography. If you have a good webcam and lighting setup at home, you can also use that and take advantage of timers.

You should wear smart casual or professional clothing, depending on your brand image. If your brand is more professional or serious, then you can also use a more serious facial expression, but be sure to get a second opinion about whether you look angry. There are very few people in this world who can hold a neutral face toward the camera and not have it come off as either creepy or angry.

Naturally, smiling is best. Although a potential company will interview you for your skills and value, they also need to be able to imagine working with you every day. A smiling face means they're more likely to imagine positive interactions with you. As a newcomer to tech, you need to be open to frequent and plentiful criticism, so a smile also provides a feeling of being open and willing to listen.

Take advantage of real-world meetups by taking photos of them and having others take photos of you there, too. Having a picture of you at a hackathon or talking to a group of developers is unlikely to work as a profile picture, but you sometimes get lucky. A backup option can be to use it as your cover photo.

Many people who aren't confident in their appearance will do anything to avoid the advice to use a photographer or to post a real photo of themselves. Trust me when I say that this is not a competition about looks but rather about putting your best foot forward. The use of cartoon avatars, emojis, and logos is fine for casual social media use, but our goal here is to provide a profile for your future coworkers and employers, and they want to be able to picture saying hello to you in the morning. Try to make that as easy for them as possible!

I will say, there's an exception here for those hoping to go into Web3, crypto, or NFTs, as the use of cartoon avatars there is often a mark of being part of that crowd. It's not my area of expertise, but as always, my advice would be to research some of the bigger accounts in that niche and pay attention to what the trends are.

Short Description or Byline

On platforms like Twitter, Instagram, and LinkedIn, there's space for a small, character-limited description or byline. On LinkedIn, this is typically your job description (we'll get more into how you can work with LinkedIn bylines later in this section). For other platforms, though, there is a bit of an art to a good description.

Firstly, if you haven't hit your three words in your cover photo, you'll want to include them here for sure. If you've already showcased your three words, then don't repeat them. Instead, add something more descriptive about your content or about yourself. For example, I've used this space to say 'Former opera singer', 'Conference speaker', and 'YouTube creator'.

In the past, I've fallen into the trap of trying to list everything I'm interested in in this section. 'Mum. Programmer. Project manager. Dugong-lover. Australian living in Germany. etc'. It was *a lot,* and looking back, I can see how silly it was. My thinking was, 'I'm a multifaceted person; I want people to see that', which is great, but the problem becomes that of branding and memory. Just as mentioned before, we want people to come away with a solid idea of who you are, anchored in their memory with something a bit strange or different. Therefore, try to avoid too many 'fun facts' and stick to the core of who you are (as per your brand package) and what you have to offer.

This last point is something I'll come back to later, but it's important that you think about it for a while. You're likely coming at social media from a *you* perspective: who you are, what interests you have, etc. The thing is, *so is everyone else.* As a result, you need to think about what you can write in your short description that will provide value to *other* people, especially other software engineers and hiring managers. What will you tweet about? How will you make their newsfeed more interesting? Why should they follow you? The answers to these questions should form the basis of your short description.

For example, most people don't care that I love dugongs and sea cows deeply, unfortunately. To me, it seems like a critical fact: you can't know me and understand who I am without knowing that about me, and I will gladly talk about it to anyone. However, the truth is that it's just not as important to other people as it is to me. Similarly, my time as an Australian immigrating to a new country with a different culture and language was an absolutely pivotal time in my life, but again, most people on my social media aren't there to hear sob stories about the difficulties of a middle-class immigrant, because it's just not that interesting. Although I don't close off those topics, I also don't highlight them or put them forward as being key things about myself. Rather, I focus on what I can offer the reader: I give them a reason to interact with my feed and to either click 'Follow' or visit my YouTube channel.

Image: My Twitter profile at the time of writing

As a job seeker, your goal is to get people to visit your portfolio or your LinkedIn profile. If there's space for a link, make sure to focus on that. The more targeted you are in your call to action, the better. So, I'd always recommend focusing on one (maximum two) links.

Emojis can also be very effective in the short description section. I would say to use a maximum of three in this section and to use them either to express a fact about yourself (eg if you're part of the LGBTQ+ community, you could use the rainbow flag), as a unique way to style bullet points about yourself, or as arrows to links. Of course, there are no hard-and-fast rules when it comes to emojis, but in general, they can be great to catch someone's eye if used tastefully.

Long Description/About Me

Some platforms, such as Facebook and LinkedIn, offer you the option of a longer 'About Me' section. I'll keep this short because the answer here is easy: this is where you put your elevator pitch. Put it into words that are as generalised for a hiring audience as you can, and insert it here. Keep it to only one paragraph or two to three sentences with some bullet points.

Pinned Posts

Pinned posts, highlight reels, and so on are one of the biggest gifts a social network can give you as someone trying to market yourself. This allows you to control the bigger picture about who you are.

In the other sections, you're *telling* the reader who you are and what you can offer them. In pinned posts, you are *showing* the reader that you can deliver on that promise. If you can highlight multiple posts, like with Instagram's Story Highlights, try to choose those that are most popular and/or most helpful to your readers—ideally sorted into easy-to-understand categories. If you can only choose one post, such as on Twitter, pick the post with the most likes. If you're lucky enough to have multiple posts with a lot of likes, then use the one that showcases your brand to employers and other engineers the most.

In general, having a popular but uninteresting post on top is stronger than a post you *think* is a winner but that only has one or two likes. Why? Because when people see that other people enjoy your content, it acts as further social proof that you're respected and know what you're talking about. Again, since our overarching goal is to convince employers you're a minimal risk to them, this kind of social proof is invaluable.

Chapter 8

Types of Communities and Events

If you haven't had any contact or connection with the tech world up until now, it probably seems like an entirely different planet. As with any industry, from banking to automotive, it has its own terminology, figureheads, and inside jokes. Right now, you're an outsider, and you have to find a way to land on that planet and make friends with the locals. Naturally, this begs the question, 'How do I even start?'

Luckily for you, software engineers and other techies love creating communities both online and in-person. Many of them want to engage more beginners and get to know others in their area with similar interests.

Before COVID, the traditional way of doing this was by attending meetups. Meetup.com was (and as far as I know at the time of writing, still is) home of the technical meetup. I remember moving to Germany as an expat (many years before finding tech), looking on Meetup.com for other expat groups, and being constantly frustrated by how many programming-based events were on there! If you live near a city or a large town, there's likely to be at least one technical meetup in your area.

What occurs at meetups is largely dependent on the people organising it. As an example, here are a few of the meetups currently happening in Leipzig, where I live:

- 'Beginner coding sessions: Come along and work on your code with others'
- 'Expert technical talks with Q&A afterwards'
- 'Q&A sessions with locals who run coding bootcamps'

From time to time, purely social events will also be offered where those in tech can come and eat pizza and get to know each other.

Another common in-person event is the Hackathon. If you haven't heard of a hackathon, then hold onto your hat. A hackathon is usually held over a weekend or two-day span. People are sorted into teams, and each team has the challenge of developing some sort of solution over the two days, such as building a piece of software, designing a website, or maybe even just coming up with a technical strategy for a business. Hackathons are known for being extremely intense, with participants often barely sleeping and just trying to crank out as much code as possible in 48 hours. 'Hacking', it should be noted, is referring in this case to 'hacking away at the keyboard' (ie typing vigorously) rather than 'hacking into a system'. At the end of the hackathon, participants present their results to the other teams.

Hackathons have been known to form the basis of a lot of great ideas. They inspire creativity, get people excited about code, and bring the diaspora of tech closer together—sometimes literally. When I was learning to code, attending a hackathon was *the* suggestion I kept seeing for connecting with the community. I found this frustrating because, as the mum of a baby, there was no way I could just disappear for 48 hours while she was still breastfeeding. I was also at the start of my time learning to program and was terrified I would arrive at the event and be useless to my team.

Luckily, meetups and hackathons aren't the only way to build a network. Due to the huge digitalisation push caused by the COVID pandemic, there are many more options available online and fully remotely now. There are even options for those who can't attend events at set times.

Conferences are traditionally held in person, but are now often online or offered in a hybrid format. Conferences are a great way to expand your mindset and learn about new and emerging technologies; however, I would argue that, for beginners, they're not often as useful, as they'll talk on a level you likely haven't reached yet. That said, several conferences are geared toward beginners or have a 'beginner track' where they purposefully keep the topics more simple and straightforward.

If you do want to attend a conference for the networking benefits, I strongly recommend trying to attend in person rather than online. When you're in person, there's a chance of sitting next to someone and striking up a conversation that could change your life or make you a new best friend. Online, you're more likely to engage in text conversations or formal Q&A sessions. Can you make contacts and broaden your network that way? Yes. Will it be as casual and easy as attending in person? No.

Online meetups, in contrast, tend to be a bit more relaxed. Since nobody comes to a meetup seeking a super sleek, professional experience, the vibe is looser and the people are readier to talk casually and honestly rather than trying to deepen their technical knowledge or investigate a new tool for their work. There are exceptions, of course, but in general, online meetups are just as pleasant as they are in person. For those who have any sort of social anxiety or who find social situations stressful, the ability to attend the session from home (and leave whenever you want to) can also be a massive benefit.

Perhaps you don't want to (or can't) actively talk to people in real-time at all. Perhaps you'd prefer a way to connect with other developers purely via text-based communication. You're not alone! There are plenty of developers who feel the same way and, due to time or preference or life circumstances, prefer asynchronous communication.

In Section 1, I mentioned that The Odin Project had a wonderful Discord community. They're not the only ones! Discord is beloved by gamers for its anonymity, and that's the reason many programmers (who tend to also be more wary of online privacy and data) are drawn to it. On the other hand, Slack is a platform used extensively throughout the tech world, including by most companies as part of their day-to-day workflow. Before programming, I had never heard of Slack. Today, I can't imagine a workday without it.

There are Slack and Discord communities for every type of programmer, and many are specifically for programmers of different demographic groups as well, such as career-changers, women, people of colour, religious groups, particular geographic regions, etc. Many influencers have their own Discord communities where like-minded followers can make the jump from Twitter, Instagram, or YouTube comments into actually getting to know each other on a deeper level.

Finding these communities can be as simple as a Google search (eg 'Discord programming servers') or they can be found via recommendations, social media, etc. Later in this section, I'll cover some dos and don'ts of social media that can also be applied to any community you join. However, the short version is that the more time and effort you spend in these communities, the easier it'll be to find contacts who can become friends.

Ideally, any community you join will have a combination of other beginners and more experienced developers who you can learn from. In a best-case scenario, you'll find a mentor who believes in your ability and hooks you up with a job once you've learned a sufficient amount. The worst-case scenario is that you don't really vibe with anyone and you end up leaving the server. Most likely, it will be something in between: you'll find a few people you connect strongly with and a lot of people you don't connect with at all, but you'll learn a lot along the way and get a feeling for what problems and issues are relevant to the tech community. Regardless of the outcome, you'll hopefully learn some of the classic inside jokes, such as not deploying your code on a Friday and that CSS is like adjusting old-school blinds.

Chapter 9

The (Mostly) Unwritten Rules Of Coding Communities

As with any community, there are some basic etiquette guidelines and assumed rules that govern a lot of online tech spaces. I'll try to keep this section short and sweet because, as with life, the most basic rule still governs: 'Do unto others as you would have them do unto you.' In other words, be polite and friendly. Those two things will get you a long way.

Beyond that though, here are some rules you should consider before engaging in a coding community, especially when using that community to help you with programming or technical problems.

Read Their Rules And Guidelines

Almost every community will have its own rules, which may or may not exist in the other communities you frequent. This is why it's important to get to know each community on its own merits, get a feel for how they work, and carefully read their rules, *especially* if you're thinking of posting something that could be considered commercial or self-promotion. For example, many communities don't allow you to share your own YouTube videos out of context, but sharing them when someone specifically asks for recommendations is OK. Other communities have no problem with videos whenever and wherever as long as they're generally relevant.

If your community doesn't seem to have any rules, but you still want some general guidelines about how to behave, a common code of conduct used in programming communities is called the Contributor Covenant code of conduct. Plug it into your favourite search engine, click on 'Latest Version', and you'll see the general principles that guide many online networks in particular.

Don't Ask To Ask

In the real world, it's common to open a request for help with 'Hey, can you help me with something?' However, in the programming world, this is generally considered a no-go. Instead, it's better to assume that everyone reading is willing to help you and jump straight into the question.

Provide Code Examples

An extension of the above rule is the consensus that any question about code should be accompanied by an example. There are a myriad of easy code-sharing websites. These sites are designed so that you can paste your code in; see the results of that code; and then share that code with others, who can, in turn, also change the code and see the results. In other words, they can actively debug your code on their own computers.

Once you've learned some programming basics, I would recommend checking out the following (or similar) sites and trying them out. You'll probably find that one or two feel easier than the others; feel free to use those ones when asking about coding problems.

Code-sharing websites:
- CodePen
- CodeSandbox
- Replit

If you need to share long text (eg a very long error message), then you should use an easy text-sharing service such as Pastebin.

Outline What You've Already Tried

Another clue for programming problems is to outline what you've already tried. Although there's no hard-and-fast rule for when you should ask for help, I would recommend trying at least two or three different ways to solve your problem before consulting the community. This not only allows you (and potential helpers) to save time by avoiding solutions you already know won't work but also allows the community to see what level you're at before they jump in. This can help avoid people talking way above your level as a beginner, which can be very intimidating.

Of course, if you're really lost and have no idea where to start, you can also say that!

Be Honest When You Don't Understand

I have mentored, led, taught, and tutored many junior developers. The absolute worst thing for me is thinking someone has understood our conversation when they have, in fact, been dishonest about their level of understanding in order to seem polite and not upset me. I understand the urge to do this, but as a teacher, it's extremely frustrating because it's a waste of my time when my students aren't learning anything.

It may feel awkward at first, especially if you're not used to admitting weakness or have a personal hang-up about looking ignorant, but the truth is that everyone's time is much better spent if you stop someone early on in an explanation as soon as you no longer follow.

If you're someone who needs examples, here are some that I use when I don't understand:

- 'Hold on a second, do you mind if we go back a few steps? I understood when you were talking about ABC, but when you mentioned XYZ, I got a bit lost.'
- 'Can I stop you there for a moment? What do you mean by XYZ? That's a new term for me.'
- 'Can you explain more about ABC? I haven't worked with that technology/tool before and the concepts around it are still unclear.'

Accept Criticism Gracefully

On a similar note to my advice on imposter syndrome, programming is a tough career for those who don't enjoy constructive criticism. Most programmers get feedback multiple times a day about ways their code could be better. When asking questions, you must be prepared to be wrong about your assumptions, realise you've misunderstood an idea, or see you've been derailed by a misplaced semicolon. None of this is a reflection of your intelligence, and getting defensive or offering lots of excuses isn't going to make your work better. But it is going to make others dread working with you. It can be emotionally difficult to deal with constant feedback like this, but the sooner you learn to accept it gracefully and move on with the important business of learning, the better your outcomes and your teamwork will be.

Bonus Tip: The Rubber Duck Technique

I couldn't finish writing this chapter without throwing in a fun bonus tip for you—the famous rubber duck technique! Once you enter programming communities, you'll start to notice an abundance of duck themes, such as rubber ducks on desks, next to monitors, on top of printers, used as logos, or flashing across your screen in YouTube videos. So why are programmers so into these little yellow ducks?

It all has to do with debugging. The idea is that when you get stuck on a programming problem (or really any sort of logical challenge), you go over the idea in the simplest language possible by…explaining it to a rubber duck. Yes, really. You literally pick the duck up in your hand and talk to it like it's a truly adorable duckling or a small child. For example, 'Well, duck, what I'm trying to do is have this button turn green when you click it. I can see that clicking the button is triggering my function, but the function doesn't seem to be impacting its colour.'

ANNA JEAN MCDOUGALL

By breaking down a problem into its most basic parts, you can hopefully find obvious logical gaps, new methods to try out, or some important aspect you may have missed. As silly as it sounds, this technique will work wonders for you, especially as a beginner to intermediate coder. It's also great practice for learning exactly how to ask questions in a programming community! Break problems down into your goal behaviour, what you've tried, and where things are going wrong, then pair it with a link to a code sample, and you're ready to roll!

Chapter 10

Mentoring and Coaching

There's a strong chance that this book isn't the only thing you've read about learning to code or changing careers and getting into tech. You've likely read or watched plenty of advice pieces and are, therefore, well-informed that 'getting a mentor' is one of the core pieces of advice the internet likes to throw at beginners.

Although having a mentor is great, this singular piece of advice can be damaging in terms of how it's presented and the impact it can have on how newcomers think. It did for me. When I first started casting around for ways to start learning to code, I struggled with motivation and consistency—I didn't have this book or the tools I offered you in Section 1, and I didn't know of any communities where I could even ask about them. Instead, I came up against this singular piece of advice time and time again. As a result, I decided the only way I could learn would be to have someone looking over my shoulder, checking in on me, and giving me 'homework'.

The above scenario is not uncommon, and I often find that those most directly looking for mentors are those who are brand new to programming. I would argue that this is, in fact, not the best time to get a mentor. Furthermore, the kind of relationship I described above isn't even one of mentorship, it's one of coaching. Let's explore what each of these are, when they're most useful, and how to find them.

Mentorship vs Coaching

'Mentor' is often thrown around as a catch-all term to mean 'a professional relationship with someone who has more experience than you'. Although it's great to surround yourself with those who are better than you, that alone does not form a mentorship.

Mentorship is a relationship in which two people share their career trajectories, goals, and personal lives. Usually, the mentor holds a position the mentee would one day like to hold. The mentor then uses their experience and story to help guide the mentee when they face situations they can't yet handle or to provide clarity for questions that the mentee might have about the industry. In programming, a mentor might jump in to help when the mentee reaches a problem they can't solve or a bug they can't fix. They could do some pair programming (when two people work on a problem at the same time) and then talk about why a certain solution worked or why another solution wasn't ideal.

Coaching has a similar premise but a different execution. Coaches usually have significant experience in the field but specialise in navigating a course for the student. Coaches can sit with their student, hear about their goals and needs, and then plan out how they get there. They identify points of weakness that the student might have and then give them ideas and exercises for how to work on those points and bring them up to an acceptable level. Usually, a coach is someone who will assign work for the student and can then check that work. It's a more formal, goal-oriented, and structured relationship.

For example, this book acts as my way of giving you career coaching by providing guidelines, exercises, and practical tips for how to reach a goal. What a book can never do is be a mentor, someone to jump in when you have a problem, respond to any personal struggles you might be going through, or carefully consider your life situation and how it influences your learning. It's impossible for a book to provide that level of personal detail and care. This is precisely why a good mentor is so valuable. However, it's also why getting a mentor early on isn't necessarily what you need—usually, what you're really looking for is a coach.

So When Should I Get a Mentor and How Do I Find One?

If you're past the growing pains of learning the basics of a programming language (ie loops, arrays, and if/else statements are easy for you to both understand and manipulate), then you have enough raw programming knowledge to start working with a mentor. Since a mentor is there more as a support and an uplifter than an actual course-setter, you're probably already on a good path of learning but need someone to check your work from time to time, offer suggestions for improvement, etc.

I'm a strong believer that finding a mentor should be a mostly organic process. In other words, you enter a community of some kind, get along well with someone in particular, and it develops into a mentor-mentee relationship over time. I've already provided tips for getting involved in communities, the rules and guidelines to follow, and the lines not to cross. As you get to know the other members of your community more and more, you'll find that you'll start to understand which people hold which interests, who has more (or less) experience, and who you personally 'click' with.

This last point is, perhaps, the most important of them all. The vibe you have with someone else is unquantifiable, unpredictable, and the most difficult part of trying to find a mentor without a prior connection. By having a casual friendship slowly evolve into that of a mentor-mentee relationship, this factor is a given. If you go to a search engine and type 'programming mentor free', then it will yield more immediate results, but it will be a more formal process, and there's a risk that it will take you many hours of 1-on-1 chats with strangers until you find someone you click with.

If you follow the more natural path of developing friendships and growing them, you might find that you end up never formally establishing a relationship with someone as a mentor and mentee. Many senior developers will assert that they don't have time for such a relationship, but will gladly chat with you in your chosen community whenever you need help. In the end, you can reap the same rewards from that kind of friendship as you can from a more formalised one.

An example of this is when I began learning to code. I was completing my #100DaysOfCode by following The Odin Project, and I was deeply involved in their Discord community. Every day, I would be there, asking for feedback while also starting to help others who had just begun. Over time, one of the senior developers and I began to chat. He sent me a blog post relevant to a question I asked and then we started talking about the situation in Germany with regards to the tech skills shortage and why I had decided to try programming, as well as his advice in terms of developing skills and looking for internships. We never formally became mentor and mentee, but his advice helped me greatly, and I knew he was always there if I became stuck.

How to Benefit from a Mentor

Whether you find a mentor by naturally developing friendships or by searching, try to keep the following tips in mind:

1. **Get to know their story:** Understanding your mentor's story is crucial to knowing what kind of questions they can best help with and ensures that you can talk to them on an equal level.

2. **Be open and honest about your story:** Are you getting into programming purely for money? Tell them. Is your dream job to work for NASA? Tell them. Do you struggle with social anxiety? Tell them. Hiding yourself from your mentor is a surefire way to receive advice you can't use. You need to be upfront about who you are and what you're looking for.

3. <u>Write down questions in advance:</u> It can be hard in the moment to really remember exactly what coding problems you've had in the last week or two. Writing down problems or questions as you encounter them means that you can come to a session prepared.

4. <u>Establish the parameters of the relationship early on:</u> Can your mentor meet once a week, once a month, or flexibly? Do they want to help with career questions or only coding questions? Do they prefer to have video calls or only communicate via text? Establishing these guidelines helps identify sticking points and potential deal-breakers early on so you don't waste weeks or months miscommunicating and getting frustrated with each other.

5. <u>Keep notes:</u> Honestly, this advice can be applied to almost any aspect of your life and learning. Keeping notes helps externalise ideas, ensures you don't forget any crucial parts of their advice, and also acts as a sort of journal for you to look over in the future if you encounter any similar problems.

6. <u>Update them on your working situation:</u> Although I discourage you from ever pressuring your mentor to give you a job at their company, you can, of course, still use them to help kickstart your job search. When you're at the point of being job-ready, have your mentor help you with your application documents and find you some early leads.

There's a lot to be gained from a mentor-mentee relationship, on both sides, if it's well-defined, honest, and consistent. Although there's no need to rush into a relationship like this, and it's not essential for success, it's also a huge boon to know that you have someone in your corner fighting for you and cheering you on. Good luck!

ANNA JEAN MCDOUGALL

Chapter 11

The Special Role of Blogging in Software Development

Before entering the tech community, I associated blogging with Yummy Mummies, organic food preparation, and angsty teen journals. It was a weird blast-from-the-past sensation when I began to frequent developer communities and saw blogs being recommended. Furthermore, there were a lot of people encouraging beginners to blog about code.

At first, I thought this was purely about content creation, which is one of the main reasons it appears here in this book. However, blogging is also crucial to developer communities because of the nature of coding problems. They're often too complex to be solved in a paragraph or two, requiring more text to explain the situation, what's causing it, and possible solutions. At the same time, day-to-day coding problems are like crossword puzzles: they can often fit neatly into one 'box' and don't require a whole book to explain.

A single blog post provides the perfect venue for developers to explain their solutions to the problems they face: an open space with the ability to add pictures and links while still compartmentalising the issue into an easy-to-understand title. You'll often find that your favourite people to follow on social media also have blogs and that the problems you search for will be answered with blog posts.

So, if developers use blogs daily to solve questions and discuss issues, should you have a blog too?

Simply put, my answer is 'Yes.' Having a long-form space for you to explain concepts, demonstrate solutions, or even just provide 'Top 5' or 'Top 10' lists is invaluable. Not only does it allow you to seamlessly integrate into the developer community by providing value to others, but it also acts as a running log of what you learn and the projects you complete. If you have a unique perspective on tech (eg by being part of an historically excluded group, having come from a different career, etc) then you can also include your observations of the community. A lot of people find new perspectives interesting and enlightening!

Of course, the most obvious benefit in a practical sense is, again, the 'social proof' you provide to potential employers that you aren't a risky choice. Blogging allows you to demonstrate the active recall of technical concepts, displays a willingness to share that information with others, and cements your reputation as someone who is *already* part of the community. In this chapter, I'll give you some reassurance about what you have to offer but also some practical tips about finding ideas, hosting a blog, and how to go about actually writing a post.

What Should I Write About? I'm Just a Beginner!

Newbie programmers are often bewildered at the idea that they have anything to offer the tech community. Part of this is good ol' fashioned imposter syndrome rearing its head, but the main misconception is the idea that you have to be an expert in something to write a blog. This idea is absolutely wrong.

Everyone has something to offer in a tech blog. After just two weeks of learning your first programming language, you'll have something you can write about. Don't worry about having to find a niche or be an expert, because tech bloggers know that a mish-mash of beginner, intermediate, and advanced techies write articles. These articles are aimed at different audiences, and therefore, different writers are expected.

Furthermore, think about what *you* want to read blog posts about. Do you want a high-level analysis of GraphQL queries and how they help in cases of over-fetching and under-fetching? Unlikely. You want to read about how to use an array method correctly, what an index is, or how someone else learned to code. Maybe you're interested in a particular book and want to read a review from other beginners to see if it's worth buying. Well, you're not alone.

As a beginner, you have a unique voice and a unique perspective. A topic may have been explained a thousand times before, but it could be that *your* explanation is the one that helps it click for a reader. As a more advanced engineer, I'm now too far removed from being a beginner to adequately explain technical concepts without accidentally using jargon. As a beginner, you're there on the ground with them. You can explain what confused you, where you got stuck, and any problems you solved.

If you look back at my old blog history, you'll see that some of my earliest posts were about basic HTML concepts. Did I say anything groundbreaking? No. Did I get numerous messages from other beginners thanking me for clearing things up? Yes!

In addition to assisting the community by adding your voice, there's also a tangible benefit to you. One of my recommendations is to use a blog as a kind of 'learning diary'. You can do this in one of two ways. Firstly, you can put aside 20 minutes each day (or few days) to explain in a blog post what you learned, any problems you had, any code samples you made, etc. Alternatively, as you're learning, you can write down 'big themes' that you encounter and learn about, then two weeks later, go back to that topic and write about it.

Both approaches have merit, but the last one is particularly effective. From a writing perspective, you have more time to marinate on the issue and really understand it. It's recent enough to be fresh in your memory while also creating enough distance that you can clearly see what you needed to learn and what misconceptions you had. From a personal perspective, this gap helps you engage in the *recall* of a topic that might otherwise start fading in your memory. That recall, as we covered in Chapter 1, is crucial for improving your technical ability.

In addition to the 'learning diary' approach, I want to offer you five other options that you can use to brainstorm blog post ideas:

1. **You: Write about yourself and your entry into tech.** What made you decide to change careers? How are you choosing to learn? How is it impacting your personal life? Do you need to quit your current job or will you learn concurrently? Are you part of a historically excluded group and have found a great community you can recommend?

2. **Interpersonal skills: Write about the non-technical skills you think others should learn.** What are you particularly good at that others aren't? What advice would you give yourself as a teenager that would make you a better student or worker?

3. **Ratings and reviews: Write about the websites, books, YouTube channels, etc that you use.** What books have you been reading? What did you like or dislike about them? What tools would you recommend to other beginners that you've found useful?

4. **Trends and predictions: Write about the future of technology.** Have you found that a lot of people are talking about some 'hot new thing' in tech and you can't stop hearing about it? What are people saying about this trend or tool?

5. **Career and work: Write about your job search and career prospects.** Once you start creating your job search package, you can

write about how it goes. What kind of job in tech would you love to have one day? What are job descriptions asking for? Which ones appeal to you and which ones don't? How are you structuring your job search? What have the interviews involved?

There are many different ways to explore and add your perspective to the world of tech. Don't be afraid to take all the things you're learning and thinking about and make them concrete using a blog post. Just remember to keep the tone interesting and (generally) optimistic.

Blog Hosting: Things to Consider

There's a running joke in the developer community that we love reinventing the wheel. Time and again, developers will make new to-do-list apps, Pomodoro timers, and…blog platforms. Many programmers love the challenge and ownership of creating their own blog to host on their own website. As a beginner, you might be tempted to take this on as a fun challenge once your technical skills are further developed. But I would encourage you to get started sooner by using one of three blogging platforms.

Using an established platform has many benefits, one of which is that search engine optimisation (ie how easy it is for potential readers to find your blog via search) is taken care of for you. Most blogging platforms also have a good sense of community, and by getting involved in that community, you can find other bloggers who write for a similar audience, see what they're doing, hit up their comments section, and more. In other words, these platforms help you build an audience for your blog.

There are three major blog hosting platforms in the developer community:

1. Medium: This is the 'big league' blogging platform, which also allows you to put a paywall on your content and make money from

your posts. I would say, however, that I've found the community aspect less exciting and the paywall keeps many readers away.

2. Dev.to: This is probably the most popular blogging community amongst developers, and it does a great job. You can add blog posts to part of a 'series', and if you first post the article on your own website, you can (and should) list the 'canonical URL' as the original site. This means that search engines will link to your website instead of to dev.to.

3. Hashnode: The new kid on the block, Hashnode has risen in popularity because it allows you to maintain all ownership of your writing as well as host the blog on your own website. It has a great community of fresh, eager writers who really engage and comment on a lot of posts.

If you want the benefit of multiple platforms, what you can do is self-host a Hashnode blog, then use that as the canonical URL for reposting on Dev.to. In doing so, you can take advantage of the communities on both while still ensuring search engines link back to your personal website. I've also posted to Medium once or twice in addition to this; however, the more places you post to, the more effort and time it takes. If technical writing is a direction you might want to go in professionally, this could be worth it for you. In the majority of cases though, double posting on both Hashnode and Dev.to will be more than sufficient.

Structuring and Writing a Blog Post

Once you have an idea for a blog post that you really like, it can be tempting to just start writing. I want you to resist this temptation until you've built a structure.

In general, blog writers tend to fall into one of two categories, both of which have problems that can be solved by structuring a blog post:

1. Someone who can write and write and write and has trouble stopping
2. Someone who struggles to put words on the page

For someone in Group 1, like me, the tendency is to ramble, get off track, or add words that are unnecessary. We tend to get side-tracked easily and want to write about every single detail of something. Although that can be nice, in general, it doesn't help when writing a blog post of about 1,000 words, because it's just *too much*. Structuring a blog post in advance allows us to stay on track, remain focused, and decide in advance what exactly it is we're going to say.

For someone in Group 2, structure offers different benefits. By taking the time beforehand to plan out your arguments, you can create a thorough enough outline to essentially make writing just transforming bullet points into sentences.

There are, of course, many different ways to structure a blog post. The easiest one to learn and master, while still being effective and feeling natural for the reader, is the following:

- Introduction: Why is this important? What will this blog help the reader learn/achieve?
- First point
- Second point
- Third point
- Conclusion: What is the main takeaway? What should the reader now know or try?

Having three main arguments/points is pretty standard, and it helps you narrow down what you're trying to say. Of course, if you're doing a 'Top 10' style list, then you would have ten smaller points instead of three larger ones, but the above structure is a great way to get started.

As an example, here is the structure for my blog post on how to give good compliments:

- Introduction:
    - Why deliver compliments?
        - Story about my friend Zach
        - How my husband gives compliments
        - Mortality: treasuring our moments with each other

First point: Why don't people give more compliments?
- Assume people already know how they feel
- Worried it will be awkward
- Don't want to seem creepy
- Don't know what to say

Second point: When should you give compliments?
- When a compliment is relevant
- Professional and work environments
- When people need a boost
- Ideally more than you think

Third point: How do you give compliments?
- Opening line:
    - 'Soft open' sentence
- Always tell the truth; always focus on the positive
- Base it on solid examples/experience you can reference
- Closing off
    - 'Soft close' sentence

Conclusion: Homework for steps to practice giving compliments

When writing, I can simply expand each of these points into a sentence or two (or, potentially, even a paragraph) and have a fully-formed blog article that stays on point and delivers key takeaways for my readers. Try doing the same, especially for your early blog posts. Feel free to go into as much detail as needed. Afterward, delete things that don't serve the main point of your post or move points around until they make sense. Once you're happy with your structure, start writing!

Once you start producing blog posts, try to release them regularly, and take the time to read other blogs on similar topics or aimed at a similar audience. This will allow you to see how others structure their writing but also gives you an opportunity to leave comments and start engaging with them. Ideally, the more you read, the more you'll understand what works and doesn't work in a blog post, which in turn will help your writing.

For the writing itself, I would argue that, although there are best practices (using active voice, avoiding ending sentences in a preposition, etc) it's far better to just jump in and start. Try to write a minimum of 500 words and a maximum of 2,000 words. Often, the shorter, more direct blog posts will get more engagement from the community because they're easier to get through, so don't feel obliged to write long-form articles every time.

English as a Second Language

Before wrapping up this chapter, I wanted to offer a quick note of encouragement for those whose native language is not English.

I recommend writing your blog posts in English because it's the international language of the internet and most programming languages. There's space for you to write in your native language too, especially if the employers you're targeting also operate in that language, but if you do that, you should be aware that you're significantly limiting your audience.

As someone living and working in my non-native language, I'm familiar with the destabilising feeling of trying to express your full thoughts in a language that doesn't match them. It can be not only challenging but extremely frustrating to feel like your points are not being fully expressed or fully comprehended.

Nothing I say here can replace the value of practice and correction multiplied by time. However, I do want to offer a few practical tools that you can use if your English isn't excellent. This also goes for native speakers who might feel uncomfortable with formal writing.

Firstly, it's a good idea to be aware of the KISS principle: 'Keep it simple, stupid.' Although the language is a bit outdated, the idea is solid: try to keep things as easy and straightforward as possible. This certainly applies to blog posts, not only in terms of content but also in terms of language. Most successful social media posts operate at about a ninth- to tenth-grade literacy level. That means that very few esoteric words are required when writing posts that others want to read. If you can't find the *exact* word you're looking for in a post, don't worry about it. Use a simple one instead and let it go. It won't make or break your post!

Secondly, I want to recommend some browser extensions to assist your English writing. You can install these in your local browser and have them automatically offer you suggestions as you write:

- LanguageTool grammar, style, and spell checker: As the name suggests.

- Grammarly: Spell checker that also gives you an idea of the tone your writing conveys (eg angry, supportive, etc)

- Ginger grammar check: Another helpful checker that also offers synonym suggestions for when you want to avoid repeating words.

Overall, the majority of people reading your blog will care far more about what you're saying than whether it's written with amazing grammar, so don't spend too much time worrying about being perfect. You're already doing a great job by reading this book in English! You can definitely write in English and produce good blog posts about what you learn: just take it step by step and allow yourself the space to make mistakes as you learn.

Chapter 12

Becoming a Social Media Hit: Building a Community by Going Beyond the Surface

The great thing about finding a coding community is that, by regularly participating, you will quite naturally start forming a network of like-minded developers. The downside is that many of these communities interact behind closed doors. That is, you often have to consciously find them and join them. Ongoing participation in a Discord or Slack community, for example, is hard to prove to a potential employer who isn't already also a member.

This is where social media comes in.

Many developers aren't the kind of people who enjoy or want to participate in social media. For some, this is because of introversion, social anxiety, or a feeling of having nothing to say. For others, it's a concern about data usage, privacy, and exposing their real name to the wrath of the internet. I understand all of these concerns, and perhaps you're just someone who will never participate in social media, but I would like to encourage you to read this chapter anyway and *then* decide.

The benefit of forming a community and/or a network on social media is the public nature of it. Simply put, the barrier to entry is small and a potential employer can, quickly and easily, see your profile and what you have to offer. This is where we go back to the concept of branding and 'social proof'. By combining your own personal brand with the public nature of social media, you can not only *tell* employers about the value you offer but *show* them the value you offer.

As a quick thought experiment, imagine again that you're working in tech recruitment. You advertise for a junior position and end up having two local bootcamp graduates apply. Their CVs are similar, but one seems to have no online presence at all (or perhaps just a stale LinkedIn page), while the other has 500 followers on Twitter and tweets every day about technical topics. This developer also has a well-filled-in LinkedIn profile that feels very similar to their Twitter feed and gives updates about their learning and links to their blog posts. You can see that other developers are chatting with them in the comments and are interested in what they're posting. Which developer do you call?

Of course, the sad reality is that the developer with no profile could actually be the more technically proficient of the two. However, there's no immediate evidence of this for the recruiter to latch onto. This is exactly what I mean when I talk about social proof. Humans are wired, to some extent, to follow and trust consensus. When a recruiter sees other developers positively interacting with your posts, it reassures them that you're someone who knows what they're doing and already part of the community. Again, this minimises the perception of risk in hiring you!

In this chapter, I'll give you my five big pieces of advice for growing any social media presence. Many of these basics will be assumed for the next section (applying for jobs), so make sure to implement the suggestions as soon as possible: if nowhere else, then on LinkedIn. Building a social media presence takes time. To reiterate my comment from this section's introduction, **if you start networking on the first day of your job search, you're too late.**

Tip 1: Keep the Audience in Mind

The majority of people using social media don't have a 'following' or an 'audience' in the sense that they're using social media to engage with their real-world friends and family, to talk about topics that interest them, or as a kind of journal of their life. There's nothing wrong with this type of social media usage; however, it's not what we want when setting you up for the job search.

In order to grow a social media presence that includes lots of other developers and get that social proof, you have to purposefully tailor what you post to their interests. This doesn't mean refraining from posting anything about your personal life at all. It simply means that you should minimise those posts and make sure that the majority of what you post is either directly tech-related or at least tech-adjacent.

Just that step alone will mean that you can start engaging meaningfully with other newcomers in the field, share your struggles and blog posts, and find a decent little community. Many newcomers to Twitter, for example, will start by tweeting updates on what they're learning using the #100DaysOfCode hashtag—that's exactly how I began, too! When you start checking that hashtag, you can quickly find others who are learning similar things and facing similar struggles. Engaging with their posts by liking and commenting is a great way to begin.

However, this alone will not get you an actively participating *audience*. If you're looking to build as many connections as you can, get more readers to your blog, or increase views to your portfolio website, then you need people to want to see your content. This naturally begs the question, 'What makes people click follow or subscribe buttons?'

Well, here's the big secret: rather than thinking about what social media has to offer you, try to think of what you have to offer the world of social media.

In other words, how can you offer value to the person looking at your posts?

How can you help others learn these topics better? How can you help encourage others to keep going, overcome adversity, or become better people? How can you make others laugh?

Some of the best newbie accounts I've seen blow up into massive followings have been those that post their notes or cheat sheets online. They don't *need* to do that; after all, they already have those notes for themselves! Instead, posting their own notes leads to two awesome side effects:

1. People love easy-to-understand summaries of difficult topics and think it will help them. They will follow you to get more.

2. Those who are more advanced than you, or at a similar level, will post their thoughts or corrections. This starts a conversation and, if you're lucky, you'll pick up other ways to help you learn that topic more thoroughly.

Yet another example is accounts that specialise in tech humour, from memes to comics to dad jokes. If you're someone who loves memes or can draw or is particularly funny, then you might choose to take this route and adapt your branding kit from Chapter 6 accordingly.

If you want to get better at producing this kind of content, then get used to thinking about the following categories every time you're about to post something. Ask yourself which one your post fits into:

1. This post provides value to an audience of other developers.
2. This post supports my branding.
3. This post is purely for me and my benefit.

You always want the majority of your posts to fit into Category 1. If I were crafting an ideal social media profile, I would probably have:

- Category 1: 75%
- Category 2: 15%
- Category 3: 10%

Even when providing value, it should still be 'on brand' for you. For example, if you as a person tend to be quiet and serious, then you should post content that represents that by focusing on blog posts, technical concepts, and (potentially) the struggles of introverted developers. You shouldn't post motivational memes, uplifting quotes, or jokes. In other words, don't try to be anything you're not. There are plenty of different personalities in the tech world, and there's space for each and every one of us to offer something unique and valuable without having to fit into a certain mould.

The only exception to this is that positivity always does better long-term than negativity. If you need to use social media to vent about the job search or how hard programming is, then I would say that post falls into Category 3. These posts are fine from time to time, and in my opinion, are also *super important* to show the difficult/human side and not engage in toxic positivity. However, start posting this kind of thing a lot and people *will* unfollow or unsubscribe. These posts should be there to help support you in your time of need and also show others a bit of the human behind the social media curtain. But, if possible, you should avoid making it your entire online persona in the long-term.

Tip 2: Stop the Scroll, Use a Hook

While Tip 1 encourages you to think about how people *view* your posts, it's also worth considering how people *find* your posts. The broad majority of the time, they'll be scrolling. They might be scrolling through a newsfeed or a recommendations list or search results, but social media is built upon scrolling.

Your goal with any post is to make it appealing enough to stop the scroll. There are many ways to do this, for example, with a great photo of yourself, a graphic of a technical concept, or a preview thumbnail for a blog post or video. Regardless of graphics, however, you should always have some type of text that acts as a 'hook'.

Compare the following two tweets. They communicate the same idea and offer useful advice to the reader, but one is ten times more popular than the other, despite being posted by a significantly smaller account.

Tweet 1:

Don't try to tick all the requirements from the job ads.

They're for the perfect candidate that only exists in job ads! Apply even if you do not meet all the requirements.

I never met them 100%, and I couldn't have learned everything I learned on the job by myself.

Tweet 2:

Apply to jobs when you meet 50% of the 'requirements'.

That's it.

That's the tweet.

If you haven't already guessed, the second tweet won with over 600 likes and over 100 shares. This isn't some magic, it's purely about stopping the scroll. Where Tweet 1 looks like a lot of text, Tweet 2 is something people can read quickly and easily. In addition, it has what I call a 'late hook', which is the 'That's the tweet' line. Another example of the 'late hook' is 'Thanks for coming to my TED Talk.' These phrases are short and familiar and grab

143

those who are scrolling because they'll immediately recognise them and go back to see what they're in reference to.

Example of some more traditional 'early' hooks include:

- 'As a developer, do you ___ ?'
- 'I achieved ___ in ___. Here's how…'
- 'Guess what? ___.'
- 'Unpopular opinion: ___.'
- 'When I was ___ I learned a lot about ___.'

Whenever I can't think of the right hook for a post, I default to some pretty blunt instruments, such as 'HEY, YOU! YES, YOU THERE SCROLLING!' which, surprisingly, does actually work.

As you can see, the goal is to pique someone's interest enough to make them stop and read your post. The ideal situation is that they really read it, read responses to it, add a comment of their own, and share it. However, even if your hook is just enough to get you a few more likes, the algorithms used by social media platforms will reward this engagement by showing your post to more people.

To put this into practice, try to check that your post has a simple, straightforward hook at the beginning or the end or as overlaid text on a video or thumbnail. Ask yourself, honestly, if you would stop scrolling to read a post like that. If in doubt, try rewriting the same idea differently once or even twice and ask a friend or contact what they think. I've used some of my Slack communities to help me test tweets in this way before. If you've made any other newbie developer contacts, they'll usually be happy to offer an opinion.

Tip 3: Engage with Big Accounts

A question I often receive is how to even *find* other people who have similar goals to you. We'll talk about hashtags and keywords in the next tip, but the absolute best way to find a quality community of like-minded developers is via already-popular accounts. When you first start looking into tech Twitter, for example, you'll quickly find names that are mentioned everywhere. Big accounts have roughly 10,000 followers or more and are so well-established and active in the community that you will quickly and easily find them.

Once you find a popular account, look through their feed and see if they have similar interests, a similar personality, or a similar level of ability to you. If so, follow them and try to visit their posts regularly (even if they don't come up naturally in your feed). Your first thought when reading this advice might be that you want to catch the attention of the big account. Although that is great if and when it happens, that's *not* actually your goal. The goal is to find other people also following this big account and convince them to follow you as well.

Here are three of the best ways to engage with big accounts:

1. Comment beyond the basics: Many people know that engaging with big accounts is a 'growth hack', so they drop 'Great post!', 'Totally agree!', and 'Nice one!' on dozens of accounts. I would recommend against this. Instead, focus on quality over quantity. Leave a two to three sentence response about how that post is relevant to your story, how it's similar to advice you give, or why it's important for people to notice. (eg 'Great post! When I was working as an opera singer, I saw the benefits of consistent practice, and the same thing ABSOLUTELY applies to programming as well.')

2. Like and respond to comments that don't have much interaction: Plenty of other people also want to find a community online and are trying to find their people through big accounts. If you see others posting and not getting many or even any responses, take the time to

respond to them, ask them questions about their experience, and see if you have any common ground.

3. <u>Share the best posts with your comments</u>: On Twitter, this would be a 'quote retweet'; on LinkedIn a 'share'; and on YouTube, it might be your own video reviewing a few other videos on a certain topic. Either way, acknowledging the effort of these accounts and then talking about how and why you liked them is a great way to give credit where credit is due but also to add your own spin to what everyone else is talking about.

If you do these steps consistently, you'll quickly start recognising other names, faces, and accounts and find that they begin to follow you. By also engaging with those accounts in the same way as the big accounts, you'll quickly find your own network of like-minded developers forming.

Tip 4: Use Relevant Hashtags and Keywords

Another quick and easy way to find accounts relevant to your journey is to use keywords and hashtags liberally. Bigger accounts often stop doing this because they grow to have so much reach that they don't need the extra boost hashtags give. But as a newcomer, you should absolutely feel no guilt about using hashtags. On Twitter, one or two is sufficient. On LinkedIn or Instagram, three or more is A-OK.

When starting out in tech, the two most popular hashtags are #100DaysOfCode for daily learning updates and #CodeNewbie (or #CodeNewbies). There are also group-specific hashtags (eg #WomenInTech, #BlackWomenInTech, etc) and, of course, hashtags for most programming languages or tech specialties (eg #JavaScript, #CyberSecurity, etc).

In addition to using these hashtags yourself, you should, of course, be using them to find others who post about similar areas of interest. Go into the search function and search for hashtags that interest you, sorting by latest or newest if possible. Just as in Tip 3, it's often the smaller accounts who appreciate interaction the most, but posting valuable comments on big accounts is also a great way to get noticed in the wider community.

Tip 5: Use Private Messaging

Sometimes, as you begin connecting more and more with people in the community, you'll find that your conversations might require longer-form communication, or perhaps you want to talk about private issues (eg talk in more detail about a failed job interview). In this case, it's absolutely okay to DM (direct message) someone you've been communicating with, assuming their account is open for DMs.

Here are some guidelines for sending DMs:

1. If you don't already know each other through many interactions, check if they're okay with you messaging them.

2. Remember the 'Don't ask to ask' rule? Don't open a DM with 'Hey, can I ask you something?' or worse still, just 'Hey' or 'Hi.' Instead, just write three to five sentences about why you're messaging them.

3. If you want to write to someone just to show appreciation, that's *great*: 'Hey, I just wanted to let you know that I love the work you're doing here on Instagram for the community. Keep it up!'

4. If you want someone to be on your channel, do an interview with you, or something similar, be prepared for them to ask if you'll

be paying them. Many social media big shots do it for a living and can't afford to take free gigs. If you can't pay, be open about that from the beginning.

5. If someone doesn't respond to you, it's okay to send *one* follow-up message after a few days.

6. If someone still doesn't respond to you, take it as a 'no' and move on.

7. …If someone directly says 'no', move on.

8. Don't DM people looking for money, follows, or gifts.

9. I hope I don't need to say this explicitly, but don't DM people trying to get a date or nudes.

You might be surprised how many people DM me looking for advice and then get *angry* at me for not answering them within an hour or two. Remember that accounts big and small have lives outside of social media, and them helping you is a kindness, not a requirement. Be friendly and open but also prepared for the fact that they just might not respond for a myriad of reasons.

There's also another way to use DMs that I've found particularly helpful over the years: group chats. Not every platform is good for group chats, but Twitter and LinkedIn can both work as ways to have ongoing communication between a set group of people. I have one group chat that I've been in since my first few months on Twitter, and we still talk every day about our personal lives, development, and Twitter itself. Another Twitter group chat eventually turned into its own Slack channel where we talk about all the things we can't post publicly about: new jobs, divorces, disputes with bosses, health issues, and more.

You might be thinking 'Why would I talk about personal issues if I'm looking to grow a tech community?' Remember that a network isn't just about a practical exchange of skills and trades but also about *people*.

Connecting well with other people, learning about their struggles, and finding ways to lift them up all help you to become a better colleague and quickly and easily find help with technical topics when you need it. All of the above groups have also helped each other solve bugs, get a better understanding of best practices in code, and provided basic overviews of new tools.

The point is that online technical conversations are built on a basis of trust and friendship, just as many workplace conversations are. Think of social media and developer communities as early practice for the workplace. If you're lucky, you'll not only become a better developer but also a better colleague.

Key Takeaways

By now, you should have a good idea of *why* crafting a solidly branded social media profile is important. Put simply, **technical skills go to waste if nobody takes an interest in you**. Nobody will check your code, look at your portfolio, or consider you a serious candidate if there isn't some sort of *proof* that you're worth talking to. Don't underestimate the role of branding, networks, and recommendations in standing out in the job market, especially if you don't have a computer science degree to back you up.

In this section, we looked at how you can boil down what makes you special into a few keywords and concepts and then repurpose that both for an 'elevator pitch' about what you bring to the table and to craft great social media profiles that allow you to display your unique personality while portraying yourself as a less risky choice for potential employers. These branding activities may make you feel a bit weird about 'selling yourself', but they're also extremely effective and give you the upper hand in comparison to the broad majority of newcomers to the field.

Luckily, even if branding isn't your strong suit, there are many different ways you can engage in the tech community and play to your strengths, from in-person meetups to Slack groups and social media platforms. By focusing on one or two of these methods and consistently connecting with other people on a personal level while offering them some sort of value, you can build a network and find other like-minded individuals.

If you're lucky, one such like-minded individual could connect with you on an even more significant level and become a mentor. This mentor-mentee relationship is a great way to deepen your knowledge of a field and will allow you to have a go-to person for any doubts, questions, or concerns you may face as you begin your new career. Of course, even without a mentor, there are still many opportunities to grow your network and provide 'social proof' that you're ready for a career in tech.

In this section, you also had a chance to learn about the special role of blogging in the tech community. Not only did you see why blogging has remained a force for inter-developer communications over the years, but you also got a clear understanding of why it's useful for you as a newcomer and the many ways you can use blogging to share what you learn. The intersection between blogging and a strong presence in the online tech community is undeniable. Having that content on call for future social media posts gives you not only great ways to share your expertise in the short-term but also provides a lot of evergreen content (i.e. content that is always valuable and not tied to a particular time period) for down the road. For example, I still regularly share my 2020 blog post about getting started using Git.

Lastly, you learned all the tips for social media engagement that took me years to learn through trial and error: putting the audience first, using hooks, engaging with big accounts, and using hashtags and private messaging to your benefit.

Most importantly, it would be impossible to do all of these steps for more than one or two social media platforms while also learning to code, especially if your time is limited due to family or work commitments. Be sure to integrate these ideas into your learning plan, spend half an hour to an hour each week on planning out your posts for the coming days, or simply try to keep the tips in mind as you engage more naturally.

Regardless of the extent to which you use this section, simply acknowledging the importance of social proof in mitigating how risky you seem is crucial. By putting yourself out there and connecting with other developers, however you choose to do it, you're building a safety net around you, a net that can catch you when you fall and that can work to lift you up when you need it.

By building this network early and caring for it regularly just as you would care for a plant, you can help it grow well before the time comes for your job search. Once the job search begins, you'll quickly see how beneficial a solid network can be. In Section 3, we'll look at when to start taking those steps and what you'll need to do to leverage your network and your social media presence to find your first job in tech.

Section 3
How You Get There

Applying and Interviewing for Jobs

Being a good tech colleague is about more than just writing good code. Hiring managers aren't usually looking for the best programmers with the best skills, but rather a combination of skills and the ability to work with others. The importance of developing the skills from both Section 1 and Section 2 of this book can, therefore, not be overstated: learning to work with others, communicate your story, and collaborate technically is crucial. However, what we still haven't covered is how to transform these skills and ideas into a job.

Unfortunately, before you have one to two years of experience, finding a job in tech isn't as simple as dropping a CV into the right inbox and then waiting for a phone call. Finding a job *is* a job. For juniors especially, competition is extremely fierce. It takes a significant amount of time and effort, and when done right, you should also be engaging in research about each company to which you apply.

Much as you did when learning to code, you should schedule time for your job search and look for feedback on how to continue improving. Try to avoid casually browsing and applying during your downtime. This not only makes it unlikely that you'll land the job (recruiters can smell a generic application a mile away) but is also part of a 'spray and pray' approach—applying to as many jobs as possible in the hopes that one works out. I've been helping developers land their first job for years. It's consistently the case that 'spray and pray' leads to a longer job search consisting of hundreds of applications, while quality applications can often get you there in under 50.

Despite the job market for developers being hot for a few years now, there are some additional hurdles for those trying to enter. As someone new to this career and unlikely to fit into a neat box of standard expectations for a junior developer, you have a particularly special one: people often hire people who are similar to them. I would have to fight my own biases hard if I were faced with a potential hire who was also an Australian migrant to Germany with a small child at home and a musical background. Like it or not, it's easier for me to sympathise with and want to help someone who has a similar story to mine. This hiring bias is something to be aware of but not frightened by.

Luckily, there's a lot more awareness nowadays of the benefits of diversity of all kinds, and more hiring managers are looking for 'non-traditional candidates' than ever before. I would add that if you see an indication of a company that's *not* aware of the benefits of diversity, that's a red flag. That company is less likely to be creative, modern, and respectful of different ideas. Run.

One thing almost all companies have in common, as you're no doubt tired of reading, is that they are risk-averse. Regardless of whether you fit into a neat box or not, you *will* have to work to convince them that you're either worth that risk or not a risk at all. In this section, we'll explore how to launch your job search and best utilise the network and skills you have built to effectively communicate that message with a 'job application pack'.

In addition, we'll explore *how* to apply for jobs. You might be surprised at what I recommend, but spoiler alert: it's the absolute opposite of 'spray and pray'. As with many of the recommendations you've already explored in this book, my approach takes a bit more time, a bit more courage, and a lot more effort than mindlessly attaching CVs and copy-pasting cover letters, but it's also significantly more effective, and I promise it will get you a better application-to-interview ratio.

Speaking of interviews, they work a bit differently in tech. Proving you have technical skills and communication skills takes more than one meeting, and in comparison to most other industries, the interview process for a developer is extensive and time-consuming. In this section, I'll explain the various types of interviews you might face and share some wisdom from my time on the operatic stage to help you learn to manage your nerves and effectively prepare for both in-person and virtual meetings.

By this stage, you already have all the skills you need, the content to prove it, and a network to help you hear about new opportunities or provide references. Now it's time to take the plunge and land the job.

Chapter 13

'How Do I Know I'm Ready?' Mental Preparation For The Job Search

You're most likely to read this chapter before you're ready to search for a job. Maybe you're trying to prepare in advance or get a sneak peek of what awaits you in the coming months or years. Or maybe you really are on the fence about whether you're ready to get started, and you need a nudge in either direction. Regardless, I recommend you come back to this chapter again during your job search because here we'll explore some of the mental preparation needed to weather the storm of rejections coming your way.

Unless you get exceptionally lucky, it's unlikely to be easy to find your first tech job. Naturally, you might be fearful of the reaction to your applications if you're unsure of whether you're ready or not. There's good news and bad news in this regard. The good news is that, if you're not ready, you're unlikely to receive any direct feedback at all. Sometimes you'll get a rejection email, or sometimes you won't hear anything. The bad news is that you're unlikely to receive any feedback at all. This means you're also unlikely to be able to determine why you didn't progress to the next round. Was it truly because you weren't ready? Or was it because they had a friend who also applied? Or was it because you live too far from their headquarters?

Or was it because the programming language you learned wouldn't work with their projects?

The above scenario may also trigger your impostor syndrome. 'Will I ever be good enough to get a job in this industry?' you may ask yourself. I don't know you, but I do know that the broad majority of people could apply themselves to the point of getting a job in tech. Instead of 'Will I be ready?' you should be asking '*When* will I be ready?' If you can follow the steps in this chapter, get as much feedback as possible, and apply it to your continued learning, then you'll get through it and find a position. However, you may not land a position and could burn out if you take every rejection as a personal failure, allow it to impact your self-esteem, and don't take the opportunity to learn from it.

So, what kind of signs should you be looking out for that will tell you that you're ready? In this chapter, I'll give you five strategies for determining your readiness. As with all my advice, it will require you to be brave and take risks, but if you apply yourself and are honest with your progress and learning, you will succeed.

Just Apply

Let's jump straight into the most obvious way to know if you're ready: start applying.

Applying and interviewing are skills like any other, and one of the best ways to know if you'll be taken seriously is to apply and...see if you're taken seriously. If you don't get any responses or calls at all, then you might need more time to get practical experience, rework your branding or application kit, and then try again in a few months. If you get phone calls and initial interviews, then at the very least, you've done the minimum needed to get attention and have a compelling story and a well-crafted application kit. If you're flunking the technical rounds, then you know that you have further to go with your technical development, and the tests themselves should give you a solid indication of what to work on and what skills employers are looking for.

I hope it goes without saying that 'just apply' doesn't mean to just send your kit out to anyone, anywhere, and see what happens. If you're going to take this advice, then it's important you also take it seriously: treat it like the real deal, put in the time and effort, and follow the rest of the advice in this section. Although there's no magic number of applications it should take, if you're applying, I would say that a dozen applications without any interest is a good benchmark for giving it space.

Technical Milestones

If you're in the enviable position of feeling confident about your branding kit and your interviewing skills, then you might be more interested in knowing about the technical milestones that would indicate readiness.

Of course, these milestones vary based on the programming languages and/or frameworks you're learning, but here are some of the signs I would look out for if someone were to approach me about working as a junior:

- Can you build a project without referring to a tutorial? (Search engines are OK!)
- Can you explain that code to someone else?
- Can you look at another person's code and explain line-by-line what's happening? (Again, perhaps with some gaps for specific methods you're not familiar with.)
- Can you reliably use Git to clone, push, branch, and pull code?

- Are you familiar with some of the terminology of clean code, such as DRY, KISS, or the Single Responsibility Principle?
- For front-end development:
  - Can you explain the difference between Flexbox and grid in CSS?
  - Have you used a CSS framework before (eg Tailwind, Bootstrap, Material UI, etc)?
  - Can you send a GET request to an API and use the data it returns?
  - Can you create a form and send the data in a POST request?
  - Are you familiar with the basics of at least one front-end framework or library (eg Vue, React, Svelte, Angular, etc)?
- For back-end development:
  - Can you explain the difference between a controller and a service layer?
  - Can you set up a connection to a database?
  - Could you create a game in the console?
  - Can you explain what inheritance is?
  - Can you look at a database schema and explain the relationships between entities in simple terms?

Of course, you don't have to be able to answer or complete all of these, and you certainly don't need to be able to do all of them from memory or without looking up syntax for the coding scenarios. However, the point is to be able to not only complete basic technical tasks but be able to explain and communicate those tasks to someone who might have questions or suggestions. Remember the rubber duck technique? That's what you should be using to practice these skills prior to applying for jobs.

If you read the above and think 'OK, I might be a bit rusty on some of those things, but they don't sound so scary,' then you can start applying for junior positions and internships. If you're confused, freaked out, or have a sinking feeling, then you should give it more time and add those tasks into your agile learning plan. No matter how intimidating it all sounds now, as always, the simple application of time and practice with the magic ingredient of consistency will get you there.

ANNA JEAN MCDOUGALL

Lean on Contacts or a Mentor

The technical milestones I've listed above are what I would recommend if someone asked me. That doesn't make them the 'definitive list' of what's required. That becomes more accurate the more locally your job search is happening or the more niche the field is that you want to enter. This is where your network comes in.

By now, you should have one or several communities in which you're actively participating and talking to other developers. Ideally, several of those developers are already working in the area or field you're interested in. If so, contact them to see if they'd be open to a 15-minute conversation about your progress. Tell them about what you've been learning and what you've made, and be open about the areas you think need improvement. Ask them what expectations they would have if a junior joined their team.

Of course, this is also a perfect conversation to have with a mentor. If you already have a mentor up your sleeve, then these kinds of chats should happen every few months anyway. If you aren't having these discussions regularly, be sure to bring up that you're thinking of applying for a few jobs to test the waters and see how they react. It will usually become pretty obvious what they think of the idea and your chances.

The other option is to take to social media and ask openly. By putting it out in the open, you can get more varied responses, potentially also from people you haven't met yet (hello, new contacts!) and from people who aren't worried about putting a friendship at jeopardy or making a community awkward. If you're the kind of person who needs templates, try something like this:

> *'Mid-level and senior developers: I'm learning ___ and can currently do ___. I'm still learning ___ but feel confident I'll get there soon. Would you expect a new junior at your workplace to be at a similar level? Or should I learn more before I start applying?'*

This kind of post can do really well on a platform like LinkedIn, and if you're lucky, it could even lead to someone sending you a job ad that might be at your level. Even if only one person responds, that's one more person who can provide you with the information you need to better learn the necessary skills and hone your application kit.

Reach Out to Recruiters

If you thought the last suggestion sounded scary, then this one will terrify you. Rather than posting publicly or in friendly communities, you can also search for recruiters in your area and ask them directly.

We'll talk about recruiter messages in more detail later, but for now, a simple enquiry and a request for a five-minute call should pique their interest. Treat the start of this phone call as if it's an initial interview and have your elevator pitch ready. Once you've covered the basics about you, ask for their expertise with questions such as:

- If I were applying for a position with one of your clients, would you recommend me?
- Would you expect someone at my level to be job-ready for a junior developer role?
- What skill would you recommend I learn or emphasise to put me ahead of other applicants?

You should be visibly taking notes (ie with a pen and paper, since typing can look like you're not listening) and following up with questions if you feel like there's not enough detail. Some good follow-up questions can be as simple as 'Why?', 'Why not?', or 'How do I show that in an application?'

If you can get two to three of these conversations under your belt, then you will have a huge advantage going into the job search. Do keep in mind that most recruiters won't be hired to look for juniors, so it's normally best not to expect a job to directly emerge from these chats. However, they can provide you with valuable insights about where you should be aiming nevertheless. Furthermore, recruiters will often try to keep the connection with you alive because, in one to two years, you could be the perfect candidate for a mid-level position they're trying to fill. Be polite and nurture these relationships!

Freelance to Fill the Gap

If you feel technically competent but aren't getting much interest in the above scenarios, it could be time to start challenging yourself.

In Chapter 3, I introduced the idea of 'bush bashing' as a way of learning to code—jumping into a project and learning as you go. Similarly, a great way to test if you're able to create ready-to-market products is to start freelancing. For example, if you're learning web development, you can find a friend, family member, or a local shop that needs a website. The next step is clear: you build it.

In this way, you're able to not only build up your portfolio (which we'll cover in more detail later) with a real-world example, but you can also list this as practical experience on your CV and repeatedly refer to 'working with clients' in your cover letters as one of your skills. Practical, paid experience is useful in so many ways, and it boosts your applications by enabling you to use numbers and facts rather than just promises of your potential. To reap the benefits of small freelance projects even more, offer your services to the client with the agreement that they, in turn, provide you with a written reference. You can then include this reference as an attachment in your applications as proof that you're not a risky hire.

The first projects you complete for a real-world client are unlikely to be easy, and you're probably going to need to lean on your mentor, community, and/or social networks for support to get through. But you should complete them feeling confident that you know the direction you're going in, even if the details of implementation are confusing or new to you.

However, if you find that you're *not* able to complete the project or face significant problems or delays, then you may have overestimated your technical abilities. This is why working with people or businesses with few requirements and low expectations is key. If needed, give your apologies and back out of the agreement. You may have lost the client and the reference, but you'll have learned something extremely useful about the gap between where you are and where you want to be.

One last point to consider before you start calling your friend about her new jewellery business is to be sure to check your local laws in regard to the legal or financial implications of freelancing. Some countries only require you to list the income on your tax return, others require you to apply for a freelancing licence, and others still will have you estimate your earnings in advance so you can pre-pay tax. The point is that it varies greatly between countries, and sometimes even between states, so consult with any local freelancers you know, or if in doubt, talk to an accountant.

A workaround to the legal problems that is still advantageous but not as exciting is, of course, to not charge for your services. This has the benefit of making 'clients' easier to find while still giving you a reference as well as the information you need about whether you're ready for real-world projects. Naturally, the downside is that you'll spend hours on a project you won't get paid for. It's up to you if that trade-off is worth it or not.

Chapter 14

What Jobs Are Available? Where Should I Look?

As discussed, freelancing can be a risky way to start. Most people prefer the stability and the simplicity of direct employment, that is, working full-time or part-time for a company that pays you a salary. In this chapter, we'll explore what kind of opportunities like these exist and where you can find them.

There are many different ways in which tech products, software, and code ends up getting developed and shipped to customers, and in turn, there are many different types of companies looking for software developers. Finding job vacancies for available positions will usually happen online, and it will usually happen via either a company's website or a job aggregation board. Since this latter category varies greatly based on your location and there are just *so many* of them, I won't be focusing on them in this chapter.

Similarly to Section 1, we'll instead look at your *options*. There are plenty of options in tech, both in terms of the work you do and for whom you do it. Furthermore, there are options in terms of work models, such as the physical location you work in, the way your schedule is organised, and the pay you can expect. As you'll see, every type of company hiring developers has pros and cons, but it's worth being aware of each of them so you can know where to look.

Startups

Startups are a world unto themselves. Usually, they are formed by one or two people who have an idea for a product or service. Then, with mostly private investment, they (hopefully) develop into a fully-fledged company. Along the way, many of these startups will hire developers.

This setup provides you with a lot of opportunities but also a lot of challenges.

When working in a startup, you're likely to take on a lot of responsibility very early. This can be tough as a newcomer to the industry because you're less likely to have guidance and more likely to have to 'struggle through' on your own. This kind of approach can be extremely motivating for people who love a challenge and who enjoy having ownership over their work. However, for those who relish community and want more guidance in their first tech job, this could be an intimidating prospect. Only you know which of these categories you fall into.

On the plus side, having that much ownership and responsibility provides a developer with plenty of opportunities, both financially and career-wise. For example, many startups will offer some form of equity (a share in the company's profits or financial results) to its early hires. If you, as a new employee, can secure even a small percentage and the company does well or is acquired, you could receive an enormous payout. Furthermore, as the startup grows, so too will the need for more senior developers, managers, etc. If you're a particularly ambitious person who yearns to climb the ladder, then this too presents opportunities.

Of course, with big rewards come big risks. The majority of startups don't go on to become multi-million-dollar ventures, and you're more likely to join a startup only to see it fold within a year or two. Although this might sound scary to you, don't write it off yet. Everyone in the industry understands that startups come with this risk, and nobody would look down on a developer who moved on from a failed startup. Once you have one to two years of developer experience under your belt, you might be surprised at how (comparatively) easy it is to find another job. If, however, your aim with your first tech job is to move countries (ie to get sponsorship) or to have a secure source of income over many years (eg to support a family) then a more established business might be preferable.

One further downside I should mention is that there are rarely established procedures in place for dealing with workplace conflict, harassment, etc. If you're part of an historically excluded group and are concerned about facing discrimination in the workplace, this might be something worth considering. Are you willing to be the person who forms these kinds of guidelines? Who can talk directly to a CEO when one of their favourite managers ends up being a harasser? Are you ready to have those kinds of conversations? If not, or if you're someone who enjoys having rules as a form of protection, then a startup might not be for you.

Small To Medium Tech Companies

One level up from the startup are small- to medium-sized tech companies. Unlike a startup, these companies normally revolve around a proven product, service, application, or similar. The company itself is usually owned or backed by a larger company or, alternatively, has stabilised to the point of no longer needing external financial support.

The benefit of these companies is that you can work in a normal-sized team, usually have a decent amount of ongoing support (depending on the company's culture, of course!), and work consistently on one product over time. Pay rates at these companies aren't often particularly impressive; however, you'll have a good amount of ownership over your work, and you get to dive deep into one codebase.

Aside from pay, the only other downside is that these companies rarely offer you the opportunity to explore other programming languages or areas of tech. If you're someone who really wants to broaden your horizons and branch out to different areas before specialising, then this might not be the best choice for you. If, however, you really enjoy what you're learning and are happy to stick to one thing over a longer period of time, then this could be a great option for you.

Big Tech Companies

If you haven't heard the acronym FAANG yet, then here it is: Facebook (now Meta), Amazon, Apple, Netflix, and Google. These are the 'Big 5' in tech, and correspondingly, many developers end up setting their sights on at least one of these as their dream employer. The other role FAANG companies serve is as the source of many running jokes in tech social media circles. The first is that the best thing you can do for your social media following is to fail at a FAANG interview and then report what happened: people *love* reading these stories, presumably as a way to learn and prepare for their own FAANG interviews. If you're successful, then the second joke kicks in: that everyone who works at FAANG is doing it just so they can put 'ex-Google', 'ex-Netflix', or similar on their CV and social media profiles.

Suffice it to say, it's *really* difficult to get hired by one of these companies or any similar behemoths such as Twitter or Spotify. The tech interview process for these companies (which I'll explain in the next chapter) is about twice as long and can extend into six, seven, or even eight interview stages. Yes, really.

Furthermore, once you're at one of these companies, it's easy to feel lost in a sea of extraordinary talent all fighting to get ahead and be seen and heard. At the same time, you'll be tasked with learning the entirety of a very specific programming ecosystem: many of these companies have developed their own tools and processes, and many of these won't transfer to your next job.

The reason the joke about the 'ex-Google' social media influencers exists is because so many people end up leaving and citing work-life balance as the reason. For the extremely ambitious and those with fewer familial commitments, this might actually sound like an amazing opportunity. Mostly, though, I would worry that a newcomer starting their first job in a company like this would not only feel lost but also be at extreme risk of burnout.

Furthermore, these companies *usually* only hire computer science graduates. Although some are purposefully expanding their reach in the interest of diversity, I would encourage you not to assume you will get an interview with one of these companies as your first tech job.

But, of course, it's not all bad: the pay at these companies is normally top-of-the-line. They want to attract the absolute best talent and they're willing to pay for it. Furthermore, the jokes are based on some truth: work for a few years at FAANG or similar and you can basically get any job you want.

Agencies/Consultancies

Many newcomers to tech aren't aware of the role of agencies and consultancies, but these are often some of the best places to dip your toe into tech.

Put simply, many people and companies need software, mobile applications, or websites but have no interest in creating their own IT departments. Agencies solve this problem by having specialist teams that they can bring on board for individual projects. For example, my first tech role was as a junior software engineer for a consultancy called Novatec, which consisted of about 200 developers. When a new project opportunity came along, they would provide a proposal and a quote to the potential client. If selected, Novatec would provide as many engineers as needed to complete the project within the terms of the contract. In some cases, this meant teams of 30-40 engineers. In other cases, it meant a team of one.

As a developer, companies like these provide a great opportunity. For one thing, the sheer number of developers available, each with their own specialisations, means there's always someone to help you when you get stuck. The breadth of technologies and interests is also useful in terms of exploring other avenues in case you find yourself dissatisfied with the one you originally chose. For example, you might have specialised in web development but then decide that you'd rather start developing for mobile apps. Having a company that provides both means that it's easier for you to 'develop horizontally' and learn those skills while still working rather than trying to learn them in your own time or jump to a new company to pursue a different interest.

Naturally, there are some downsides too. Firstly, you are beholden to the contracts that the company actually has. If your company doesn't have any projects that interest you, you are, nevertheless, stuck having to work on one of them. Some agencies will 'hire out' developers to other companies, meaning that, although you're working for a consultancy officially, you're *really* working for a local company and reporting to their managers. Sometimes, this even means going to work in someone else's offices with no other developers from your company itself.

When doing interviews for consultancies, it's worth asking questions about these practices. Whether such a set-up bothers you or not, it's important that you understand how your work will function. For example, although a consultancy might have flexible hours and a remote work setup, their client may insist on two in-office days with set hours. This can mean that the benefits you feel have been promised to you during the interview process can be taken away once the actual work begins. You have a right to know if this is possible so you can plan accordingly.

Normal Companies With Tech Departments

Another category of companies hiring developers are your normal, everyday medium to large businesses. Banks, car rental companies, airlines, fast food chains, construction companies, and many others will have their own IT departments with their own developers. Although many of these companies will hire consultancies to complete individual projects, they will often have a core team that works on internally developed platforms, systems, or products.

The downside of working in such a department is, simply put, that they aren't tech companies. Traditional companies tend to use traditional models of employment. You're less likely to be offered flexible hours or remote work and more likely to be required to 'clock in' and be on-site. Furthermore, agile processes are less likely to be in place, depending on who has come before you and how open upper management is to letting their developers organise their own work. Simply put, it's a gamble. Yet again, the best way to manage this risk is to just ask about the policies and culture during the interviews.

The upside of these companies actually has more to do with you and your hireability than it does with the work itself. If you're coming from a former career, and you can relate that career to a large company with an IT department, then your value as a developer increases. For example, my current position as of writing is with a subsidiary of the media giant Axel Springer called National Media and Tech. Although I entered this job with relatively little technical experience, my undergraduate degree and much of my early work was in media and communications, including journalism studies. In tech, we call this 'domain knowledge'. Having that background allowed me to argue that I was uniquely positioned to understand the challenges of the journalists and editorial teams served by the tech produced by National Media and Tech. If you can connect your former work with some sort of domain knowledge, then it's worth making that connection very explicitly in all your application documents, interviews, etc.

Additionally, if you currently hold a part- or full-time position in a large company and are a good employee with a good track record, check to see if your employer is hiring developers. They are much more likely to give you a chance if they know you're motivated, reliable, and a good colleague. If they won't consider you now, then ask what you would need to learn or show to be given a chance to switch while also emphasising that you don't want to leave the company and would prefer to continue providing them with value.

Overall, these companies are the most overlooked when newcomers are searching for jobs. That's often because they don't advertise in all the places developers expect. It's not uncommon for these companies to only list their open positions on their websites. So, do some research on medium and large companies in your area and domain and then start manually visiting websites. It's not as convenient as bulk-applying via job search websites, but as you surely know by now, the easy way is often the hardest way to actually be effective.

Chapter 15: Creating an Application Kit

Buckle up, because this is where the job search gets personal. In Section 2, we discussed your personal brand, creating social media profiles, and how to build a story around you and your value. This is where we take it to the next stage and turn those same pieces of information into the various documents and projects that employers will expect.

There are, of course, some regional variations around what's called for in an application kit or even on a CV. For example, in Germany and many other European countries, it's still expected to include a photo and sometimes even your marital status, whereas in Australia, people would definitely raise an eyebrow if you included either.

Nevertheless, there are some basics that can be applied almost universally. The theme I will continue to come back to is what I call the **'NNQ' rule: names, numbers, and quotes**. If you're ever in doubt about what to include on your application documents, this should be your fallback, and as you'll see throughout this chapter, I encourage you to find pieces of NNQ to insert at every stage.

Names are important because they help connect your application to people who already have a relationship to the company you're applying to. After all, as humans, we constantly seek connection, and if you can show a connection to someone who's 'low-risk' (eg a friend, contact, or coworker of the hiring manager), then you foster early familiarity. Which sounds stronger, 'I saw this job advertised and thought it sounded like a great fit' or 'I spoke to Janet Wong and she seemed to think this job could be a good fit for me'?

Numbers lend credibility to your claims. Unlike names, they connect to the logical part of the reader's brain and allow them to latch onto something concrete and objective. By adding quantitative (number-based) statements next to qualitative (value-based) statements, you can prove that what you're saying is true. This is the difference between 'I won most-profitable salesperson in 2022' and 'I won most profitable salesperson in 2022 by achieving 160% profit from the previous year.'

Quotes are useful for showing that you're someone people want to work with. Where names can help get an application started or pique the interest of the reader, quotes allow you to deepen the sense of value you provide. I personally think that there's nothing more valuable than quotes and references from previous coworkers, study buddies, teachers, mentors, or anyone who has experience being in a team with or working alongside you. Each quote you provide is one more data point for the recruiter to know that you're someone who will probably do well in a team.

We'll come back to each of these throughout this chapter. Naturally, you'll want to know where and how you should use them. There are three pieces to the application kit that you *must* have when applying for your first developer job:

1. CV/resume: a document describing your work history, educational background, etc.

2. Portfolio: a website, profile page, or other site where you can demonstrate your coding ability.

3. Cover letter: an email or one-page document explaining why you're applying and why you're a good choice.

In this chapter, we'll cover each of these areas, not only in terms of formatting and requirements but also how to complete them when your background isn't technical. For career changers, for example, it's often difficult to understand how much of your past work experience to include or how to connect it to your desired tech career.

In addition to this, most companies will actively hire via LinkedIn. Although we touched briefly on social media profiles, this chapter will provide some additional tips for maximising your visibility (and hireability) on LinkedIn specifically.

How Much or How Little to Mention Your Former Career

If you're coming from a different industry, it might be tempting to go with a 'clean slate' approach to a CV. Unless you're under the age of 25 or have very little work history, I would recommend taking a more nuanced approach to your former career.

There are several points to consider when deciding how much or little to mention your former career in your application documents.

Firstly, if there's no avoiding your work history, include it. By this, I mean you've worked the last 15 years in a particular industry and there's no other experience or work that you can use in its place. In this scenario, the best option is to lean into the previous job and take the opportunity to explain how the skills you learned in that career help make you a better programmer. In my case, I wrote a blog post about how opera prepared me for a programming career and linked it everywhere.

Secondly, if you can in any way link your job to the technical field, include it. This means you should automatically include any work experience in STEM (science, technology, engineering, mathematics) but also any job or work responsibilities in which you worked *alongside* tech. For example, if you created a small landing page in your marketing job, that should be mentioned. On the other side of the coin, if your previous work hired developers to create an app, for example, and you gave them specifications for what you wanted, then that's *product development experience* and you should mention that. If you were an office manager who dealt with the IT department and their server room, you can mention that.

Any connection at all to the world of product development or engineering should be highlighted. Additionally, any skills you learned in terms of teamwork, communication, and leadership should be emphasised. Remember that companies are also thinking long-term about who could eventually help lead their teams!

If you worked more than one job at a time, then I strongly recommend choosing whichever one makes you seem more technically proficient or a better leader. Along the same lines, if you were a freelancer who has completed multiple small- to medium-sized projects, then I would recommend lumping them all together into one job title/description.

The last scenario that I hear about quite regularly is that of stay-at-home parents (SAHP). Often, SAHP have taken multiple years away from the workforce, and some have never even entered the job market at all. In this scenario, I would recommend listing this time in your CV but only with a one-line job title such as 'familial responsibilities' or something similar. If you're confident in drawing a connection between your parenting skills and your programming or teamwork skills, then you can expand on that a bit in your cover letter, for example.

In general, if there isn't a strong connection between your previous career and the job in question, then the best approach is to acknowledge the facts of it briefly and directly but not to focus on it. Instead, draw focus to your learning, any of your community work or achievements, and your relevant projects.

ANNA JEAN MCDOUGALL

CVs, Resumes, and Work History Profiles

There's no document more talked about when applying for jobs than the CV. For the sake of simplicity, I'll lump anything where you have to fill in a work history into the term CV, including any online forms you might fill in or your LinkedIn profile (or similar online career networking site).

Curriculum vitae (CV) is a Latin term meaning 'the course of one's life'. Given that, you could be tempted to think this is a great place to express everything about you as a person. Unfortunately, you'd be wrong. As the standard advice goes, most CVs should be only one to two pages. Just as I said in Section 2, your job is to condense the most important information about you and your suitability for the job into this space.

Take this opportunity to go back to your branding kit and revise your elevator pitch, your three words, and your unique selling point. You should keep all of these in mind when structuring your CV and deciding which pieces of information should be included and which shouldn't.

Although we'll later investigate when and how to adjust your CV for different jobs, you should, nevertheless, have one or two 'basic' versions that can be used as the basis for your applications.

Visually Stunning vs Basic Text CVs

One piece of advice I hear over and over again from other developers is how to make your CV look great. Front-end developers in particular seem to feel a lot of pressure to create CVs that look like websites or have particularly impressive visual elements. Although I understand how satisfying it can be to see your information presented in a well-designed document, I encourage you to steer away from this style of CV.

Why? The answer lies in your target audience.

The people reading your CV are likely to read dozens of them every day. They're used to receiving CVs and scanning them for the information and keywords they really want. As someone who has done this, I can tell you that there's nothing more frustrating than a beautiful CV that makes it difficult to find any of the information I really want to know about a candidate. By using something different/unique, it may help *you* feel good about your application, but it only makes things more complicated for the people hiring you, who now have to learn the exact layout you've decided on.

Furthermore, a highly visual CV from a career changer or junior candidate can have an unfortunate side effect—that of seeming like you're covering up your lack of experience. In general, developers pride themselves on being highly logical—a huge part of our job is literally to look behind pretty things to get to the information underneath! Forcing someone to work harder to understand your history just for them to find that the history isn't particularly amazing creates a lot of work for very little payoff.

By providing a simple, straightforward Word-style document with clear headers in a single-column format, you make the recruiter's job much easier and quickly and simply deliver the information they need. You show that you have nothing to hide and that you respect their time.

The only exception I can think of to this advice is for people actually applying for a design or UI/UX position. Even then, you'll want to stick to convention as much as you can and design around that.

Make Contact Easy

A quick point that's important to make is that your CV should have all your core contact information on it:

- Address (or at least city/state and country)
- Email address
- Phone number
- LinkedIn (or other regional) profile

You would be surprised how many CVs I've seen with no email address on them! Your potential employer will send your CV at every stage of the job application process, and almost everyone you talk to will have read it before speaking to you. If they have questions, need to reschedule, or want to follow up to accept/reject your application, they'll want your contact information in that document.

One caveat: if you're going to upload your CV or link to it in any sort of public location (eg your portfolio website, your LinkedIn profile, etc), be sure to remove the contact details before uploading. Not only can harassers and identity thieves use this information against you, but there are also bots scouring the web looking for email addresses they can exploit or spam.

Structuring CVs with No Technical Work History

As I mentioned earlier, there will be many people reading this who do not have any connection to technical or leadership skills in their work history. For these people, I have three recommendations.

Firstly, change the structure of your CV. Most CV templates you'll find online put work experience at the top, followed by education and then additional skills, volunteer work, references, etc. Although you can't (and shouldn't) remove the work experience completely, try opening with skills (ie programming languages/tools), projects, and any certifications in technical areas. Then follow with work experience.

If you've done any freelancing at all, that counts as work experience and you should list it as such (eg Full-Stack Software Engineer, Freelance). This allows you to expand on what you created as a freelancer and potentially link to anything you made.

My second recommendation is to use a 'foreword' or 'motivation'. This is a short section of text you can include at the top of your CV, and it acts as a mini cover letter. Personally, I love having this available, as I assume the majority of people won't actually fully read and digest the points made in a cover letter. The 'motivation' section should use one to two sentences that hit your unique selling point and then mention what you're looking for. Of course, this is a section you should change with every new application so as to fit the job description.

Lastly, keep the CV to one page if at all possible. This allows you to use just one line to describe your previous career without it looking strange to the recruiter. If you have two pages of information about yourself but then only one line about a job you worked for seven years, it might look a bit odd. If you have only one page to cover work history, education, projects, skills, etc, it makes sense that you would condense the summary of a less-relevant job.

If you have a lot of written references (either saved or on LinkedIn), there's one final thing you can add: a page of quotes. It might seem like overkill, but the 'page of quotes' approach has worked well for me. After the CV is finished, you add one last page with 'References' or 'Written References' as the heading and fill that page with great things people have said about you using their names and current job positions. If you've sourced these from your LinkedIn recommendations, then you can use them freely, as they've already agreed to make the statements public. If you've sourced them privately (eg an email, phone call, etc), then be sure to check that they agree to you using their words and name in this way.

A Short Note on Skills

Listing out your technical skills is normal on a CV. You can quite literally just insert a list of tools, programming languages, and technologies that you know the basics of.

One trend that you shouldn't use is progress bars, percentages, or a star system for listing out how confident you are in that technology. For example, 'HTML 90%, JavaScript 65%'. For one thing, what does that even mean? What does it mean to have 65% JavaScript? Or three-star C++? Familiarity with and knowledge of technical tools is so subjective that my 65% isn't necessarily your 65%. It means nothing, and all it does is undersell your abilities.

Provide the list with no ifs or buts and let them ask you more in the interview.

Describe Achievements, Not Duties

One last major tip, which should apply to CVs everywhere, is about what to include under each job you list. It's expected that, in your work experience, you'll have two to four bullet points per job you held. The most common mistake made when writing these bullet points is to simply list what the job duties were.

For example, someone who worked the cash register at McDonald's might write:

- Taking orders from customers
- Cash and card handling
- Safe food handling

This is all factually accurate, but in a CV, *everything you write should support your application*. Rather than listing the (obvious) duties that your work involved, focus instead on some achievements. For example, we could rewrite the above with the following:

- Won Employee of the Month, April and October 2021
- Trained and mentored over 20 new employees over two years (see references)
- Attained Certificate for Safe Food Handling, February 2020

Not only does this highlight that you are skilled at working with others (training/mentoring), but it follows the NNQ rule by using numbers and quotes when referring to your references. There you can include a coworker whom you trained when they first started and who would be willing to say or write something good about your time together.

The goal here is to provide an overall image of yourself as a dedicated worker and a team player. If you can't connect your job to any technical responsibilities, then creating this impression is *crucial* in order to convince the recruiter of your potential as an employee in general.

Portfolio and Projects

A LinkedIn profile, a CV, and a cover letter are the tools you need to get you the first phone call for a job. After that, you *must* have some code available for employers to evaluate. Typically, this is done either with a portfolio website, a GitHub profile, or both.

As I mentioned in Section 1, learning Git is considered a crucial technical skill. By using GitHub consistently and uploading (pushing) your code to your profile, you should end up with a significant collection of code snippets well before looking for your first job. If you've simply been saving all your code locally on your computer, take the next few days to start pushing it all onto GitHub.

At the time of writing, GitHub also allows you to create a little 'About Me' landing page on your profile, which you can use to state your elevator pitch and summarise yourself, link to your LinkedIn profile, or direct people to read your blog or visit your portfolio site (if you have one).

In general, a portfolio site doesn't offer anything particularly unique beyond what a GitHub profile plus a LinkedIn profile can. However, there's value in having one place that's specifically all about you. A portfolio site gives you a space to describe yourself, include a contact form, link to your social media channels and/or blog, and highlight two to three projects you feel highlight your skills.

If you're pursuing a career in web development, a portfolio website also provides you with a great opportunity to hand-make your own site. When I was applying for my first tech job, I particularly enjoyed working with React. So, I built my portfolio website with React and used it as one of my highlighted projects—win-win!

Naturally, if you're more focused on back-end engineering, AI, machine learning, or similar, then you could use a no-code website creation tool (eg Wix, WordPress, Squarespace, etc) to make something using existing templates.

A common mistake I see newcomers make when creating a portfolio website is to use everything they've ever created as examples of their work. For example, many new programmers will create a Google main page clone, a tic-tac-toe game, a Pomodoro timer, a calculator, a to-do-list app, and other common projects. Listing all of these small, common projects is a waste of your valuable portfolio space.

Rather than focusing on the *quantity* of projects, try to focus on the *quality* of projects. Select no more than three projects that took a lot of time, were challenging, and for which you have worked and reworked the code many times. The code itself should be well-formatted, all the variables should be clearly named, and it should be obvious what's happening at every step of the programme. If you don't have any projects like this yet, then now's the time to start on one and integrate it into your schedule!

A great way to choose a big project is to go back to your branding kit and your CV: think about your unique selling point and your work experience and see if there's anything you could build (even if it's just a small game) that can connect these things to the kind of job you want. For example, a project I enjoyed building was a small game where users would hear two musical notes and have to determine which was higher, with infinite levels adding more notes each time. It was a silly, useless game, but it was a way to combine my classical music background with programming.

Every project you choose for this should be included in your portfolio with a preview image, a short description, a link to the deployment (ie where people can see it/play with it) if relevant, and a link to the GitHub repository where they can see the code. For anyone in web development, GitHub Pages allows you to deploy websites directly, saving you from having to buy hosting or server space.

Similarly, these projects will form the foundation of technical proof for all of your applications, so be sure to include these same links in your CV and potentially in your cover letter (especially if one of the projects matches the job description particularly well). Your portfolio and GitHub profile should also be linked everywhere: in your CV, cover letter, LinkedIn profile, etc.

One last thing to note is that projects you create via tutorials should not be included in your applications unless you make significant changes to them as part of your own initiative. Tutorials inherently end up providing you with the code, so they're not true demonstrations of what you can do when given a problem to solve. Try your best to find or create your own project idea and then code it yourself, using search engines or other developers to help you solve problems along the way, naturally!.

There are some great resources to help you further perfect your portfolio, including on my YouTube channel. Suffice it to say that there's a lot more to say, and a lot more to do when it comes to creating your own portfolio. The key is to keep it focused on your unique selling point and your technical achievements while inserting enough personality to allow people to get to know you better in the process.

Cover Letters

Writing a cover letter is a skill unto itself. Unlike your CV, there's no guarantee that anyone will actually read a cover letter. Recruiters are busy and hiring managers are busy, and they will often skip straight to the CV to get their information 'from the source'. As such, you will find many people advise you not even write a cover letter. Personally, I think that, as someone new to tech, you can't afford to avoid them.

Cover letters take time, so it's natural to want to skip over them; however, they're the one place where you have space to state your case, in detail, for why you'd be a good hire. A cover letter should be formatted like a formal letter, and the contents should describe very clearly how you match the criteria listed in the job description.

Of course, you can and should write a 'basic version' of your cover letter, which includes one to two sentences about you, some notes about your core achievements, and a written version of your elevator pitch. However, I haven't yet found two job descriptions similar enough to each other to warrant not editing your cover letter.

Simply put, every job description and every employer is a little bit different. The best cover letters I've read from applicants have been those in which it's immediately clear that the applicant has done their homework. For example, by specifically listing products/applications that my company creates, referring directly to the company values (which you can find on most corporate websites), and then directly explaining how they fit those value or how their experience would equip them to work on those products and applications.

For this reason, I like to describe cover letters as an exercise in connect-the-dots. On one side, you have dots that represent your experience, skills, and interests. On the other side, you have the job requirements. A cover letter allows you to draw lines between these items and explain how they match.

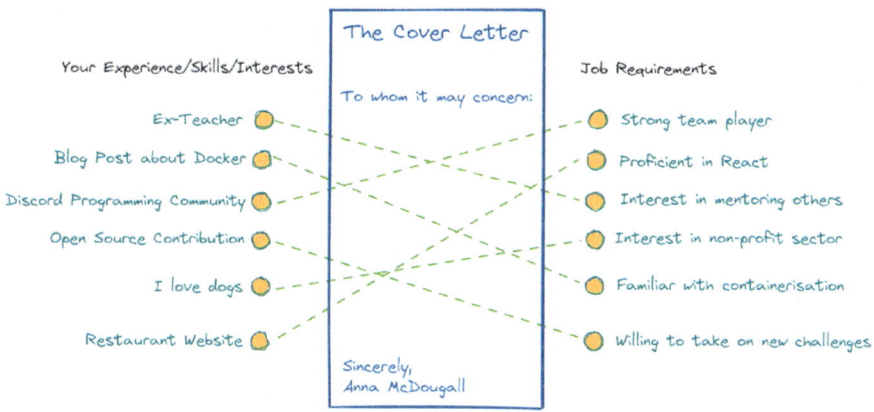

Here, you can see how, even without a degree or paid work experience, you can provide clear proof that you match the job requirements. If, for example, you feel the connection between your love of dogs and the non-profit sector isn't strong enough, then you can focus on the connections you feel *are* strong. A cover letter should, in the end, be no longer than one page, so picking the strongest connections and emphasising those is absolutely acceptable and encouraged.

I would recommend doing something like the above (on a piece of paper, in an Excel spreadsheet, or whatever works for you) for each position you want to apply for. After a while, you'll find patterns and the dots will connect more easily.

In general, this is the format you should follow for a cover letter:

1. <u>Open with a formal greeting</u>, either to the listed contact person or 'To whom it may concern' if no name is given.

2. <u>Introduce yourself</u> in one line followed by the position you're applying for.

3. <u>Connect three to four of the dots</u>, and don't forget the NNQ rule when explaining the connections!

4. <u>Mention one to two company values</u> that specifically resonate with you and your personality: this would be a good place to hit your brand words and/or your unique selling point.

5. <u>Close with how excited you'd be</u> to work with that company and that you hope to hear from them soon.

This format is simple, straightforward, and allows you to give a preview into what you have to offer while connecting it directly to the advertised job.

If you already know what the position you'll be applying for is like, then you can prepare a basic cover letter now using the requirements you think will be present. That said, remember to carefully read each cover letter before you send it out to make sure that you have written the correct company name, job title, and company values.

Using LinkedIn Effectively

Congratulations! You have your application kit: your CV, portfolio, and cover letter are all ready to be sent. However, before you begin scouring the web, there are a few specific tips I want to give you to maximise your LinkedIn profile and to give you a headstart on the job search.

Although we covered social media profile basics in Section 2, there are some changes you will need to make to your LinkedIn profile now that you're ready to look for a job:

- Use the 'Open to Work' banner: LinkedIn provides you with a great banner you can use that will overlay your profile picture with 'OPEN TO WORK'. This can be very helpful in encouraging recruiters to contact you.

- Update your job title: Remove the term 'aspiring' from your job title and instead use the job title you want followed by key items from your tech stack. For example: 'Software Engineer | JavaScript, React, HTML/CSS'. This will help you appear in recruiter search results.

- Get recommendations: It's time to source the Q in NNQ! Use the LinkedIn recommendations section of your profile to contact coworkers; friends; mentors; classmates; or anyone who can attest to your work ethic, technical skills, or learning potential. Go one step further and proactively recommend them first!

- Contact local developers: Send some messages to local developers with no agenda (ie *don't* try to find a job). Tell them about yourself and the kind of work you're looking for and ask them questions about the local job market and if there are any areas they think you should specifically work on or specialise in. If they're up for it, meet for coffee (virtual or in-person).

- Post your content: Use LinkedIn like a work-related Twitter. Post your thoughts, use hashtags liberally, and share articles you write or read that are related to tech. You can also highlight your favourites in your profile!

- Log in daily: Logging in every day keeps your profile at the top of recruiter search results. It's a small thing, but it can make a big difference.

There are many other cool ways you can use LinkedIn to get ahead, one of which we'll cover in the next chapter. However, understanding the basics is an important first step before you begin linking your LinkedIn profile throughout your application kit. Try to put yourself into the shoes of the recruiter and imagine them quickly scanning over your profile. Will they see a developer in there? Will they want to forward it on to their boss? That's the effect you want!

Chapter 16

Applying to Jobs

Now that you have an application kit that highlights your strengths, is backed up by NNQ, and utilises your branding kit, the natural next step is to apply for some jobs! In this chapter, we'll have a look at which jobs you should apply for and the two ways you can apply.

Regardless of where you find jobs—be it on a company website, a job aggregation site, or a recommendation from someone in your network—I want you to be aware of, but not guided by, the list of 'requirements' for any given position. Women in particular are prone to only applying to jobs when they meet all of the requirements. Although this sounds reasonable, what it actually means is that they're applying to jobs they're likely overqualified for.

Simply put, we as candidates read 'requirements' as 'things I *must* have', whereas recruiters and hiring managers write 'requirements' as 'things we'd *like* to have'. There's a key difference there, which is that very few requirements are really requirements at all. If you can demonstrate that you're competent in the key areas of the job and are a fast learner, a great colleague, or a solid leader, then the requirements become a lot more fluid.

As such, my rule for general (non-referral) job applications is this: **Apply to any job ad for which you fulfil 50% of the requirements.**

A fun fact I often share is that, for my first tech position, I fulfilled literally *none* of the requirements listed on the official page. Had I just applied via the company website, I would have been unlikely to get a callback. However, because I was found on social media, referred to the recruiters via the head of software engineering, and considered high-potential for my speed of learning (proven with NNQ), I was offered the contract.

It's crucial to recognise the distinction between these two standards: one for when you apply externally and one for when someone internal puts you forward. As you've likely heard time and again, most people find jobs via networking, and it's because of this phenomenon.

Fair or not, people are more likely to trust candidates who are in some way already connected to the people they know. If you're someone who's great at networking or has lots of friends or family in tech already, then this is great news for you. If, however, you're coming from a community where working in tech is unusual or you find it difficult to make new connections, then this could be news you don't want to hear. If that's the case, please go back and revisit Section 2. There are communities out there for everyone, even those who aren't comfortable with real-world events. You *can* find a network by exploring those options, talking to as many people as possible, and taking an interest in helping to lift others up as much as you would like to be lifted.

Even with recommendations, not every application will succeed. It's natural that, after several rejected applications, you will start to feel disillusioned and want to spam out the basic versions of your application documents to any job that seems vaguely suitable. I encourage you to resist this temptation and keep each and every application specific to the advertised job and the employing company.

Before I cover my application strategy, I want to add a quick note about tracking. I highly recommend building yourself an Excel spreadsheet (or your preferred method) for tracking the applications you fill out. Not only does tracking applications allow you to notice trends (What kind of companies give you a callback? What strategies got you the furthest?), it also allows you to look back at the end and say 'Whew! It took X applications, but I got my first tech job!'

The most valuable thing tracking applications provide, however, is a quick and easy reference for when someone calls you. Consider this: You spend your first week job searching and apply for 12 different junior positions. After a few days, you get a phone call from HomeTech Inc. How likely are you, in that moment, to remember which company that is and what the position's description was? What did you use as your USP? Most likely, you've forgotten and are either trying your best to silently search for the job while talking to them or simply fudging your answers to be as general as possible. Either way, you're not focused and on top of your game. Having a tracking document that you keep open on your computer (or easily accessible on your phone) is a great way to quickly look up the company and its values, the position, and one or two points about your application. This protects you for when an unexpected call arrives!

Lastly, tracking applications gives you a chance to send appropriately-timed follow-ups. My tracking document included a section for tracking the stage of each application and the last date of contact. I would also highlight the entire row in red as soon as it was rejected and orange if I thought the application wasn't going well. Green, naturally, was for the jobs that were progressing nicely every few days.

Now we can dive into the four stages of CARA:

1. Collection of information
2. Adaptation of documents
3. Recruiter contact
4. Application

By following each of these steps, and not skipping any of them, you will submit high-quality, qualified applications. It's not a silver bullet, but it will put you ahead of all the other juniors simply spamming out their documents.

Collection of Information

Once you've found a job you want to apply for, try to resist the urge to immediately send your application kit. Rather, you now need to gather information about the job, team, company, and hiring manager or recruiter. Start a new document or Notion page (or however you prefer to organise your thoughts) for each job you want to apply for so as to take notes about the information you find. For the sake of simplicity in this chapter, we'll call this document the 'job notes'.

If you've found the job on a job website (eg LinkedIn), go directly to the company website and look at the listing on their official careers page. Wherever the job is listed, be sure to check to see if there's a name for the hiring manager or recruiter and add it to your job notes. Almost always, the wording of a particular job ad will be exactly the same, but there are some differences as to how it's presented.

For example, the company website will normally provide you with information such as the company values, their statements about diversity, photos of some of the teams, and (often) some of the perks that they offer. Add anything from these pages that sounds particularly good or in line with your personality or experience into your job notes.

Company values will often be part of what's explained to potential candidates on the careers page, but if you can't find them there, then try the more generic 'About Us' page. You should read this page anyway to learn more about the company, its size, and (if relevant) its founders.

The second source of information, and in my opinion, the most important, is people. Especially for small- and medium-sized companies, it's usually easy to find a few developers working at the business on LinkedIn or even Twitter. Either way, send out a few messages—no more than two or three—to developers who seem particularly active on LinkedIn. This way, you're more likely to get a response, as many developers have a LinkedIn profile but don't really use it.

When messaging a developer, be clear that you're just gathering information to determine if you should apply. Here's an example of a message you could send:

> 'Hi Katie,
>
> *I hope you don't mind me messaging you, but I saw that you work at Amazing Tech Company, and I wanted to ask you a bit about your work there since I'm thinking of applying. What is the vibe like there? Have you found the teams to be welcoming of newcomers?*
>
> *I'd love any insights you have!'*

Ideally, this kind of message triggers a conversation about the workplace, your experience, etc. If so, be sure to thank the person for the information they give and then **ask directly if you can mention your conversation when applying for the job**. You should never use someone's name in an application unless they know about it and have given you permission, but being able to reference this conversation fits the NNQ rule and makes your application stand out. Of course, be sure to enter anything pertinent in your job notes too.

If the conversation doesn't proceed, you get ghosted, or the person refuses to let you use their name, then please be gracious and move on. You never know why someone isn't responding, and nobody owes you their time. If someone engages in a conversation like this with you, they're doing you a great favour. You can't enter these conversations with an *expectation* of immediate, enthusiastic assistance. In short, show grace.

One final source of information is YouTube. Most companies have at least one developer or business person who has given a talk somewhere—be it at a conference, on a podcast, or even a TED Talk. Finding something that's relevant to the job and referencing it in your cover letter, email, and/or first phone call is a great idea. This particular step is optional and time-consuming, so leave it for the jobs you're really excited about. However, it's also a great alternative if contacting a local developer didn't work, because it allows you to name-drop, albeit indirectly.

Adaptation of Documents

Now that you have your job notes, you're ready to adapt your CV and cover letter.

For the CV, be sure that it includes all of the relevant programming languages and tools mentioned in the job descriptions *if you've had any basic exposure to them*. Again, the list of skills should be based around basic familiarity, not mastery. You can always clarify in an interview to what degree you have worked with them.

If any of your previous work experience is relevant to the domain of the hiring company or their clients, be sure to add one or two more lines to that particular job to draw more attention to it. If there are any jobs you've left out that have domain relevance, add them back in. For example, when applying to my current position for a multinational media corporation, I added the journalism internships and volunteer work in radio I have back into my CV. For most tech applications, that experience would be irrelevant and I wouldn't include it. However, since this position involves working closely with journalistic products, data, and applications, it suddenly became relevant again.

Lastly, check the 'Motivation' section at the top of your CV. Ensure that the position you describe looking for matches the position advertised. If there's a particular perk they mention (eg flexible working hours), then describe that as something you're looking for. It gives the recruiter a feeling that this is a good match. Furthermore, see if you can work one or two of the company values into your description of yourself or your work.

Before you begin your cover letter, complete the match-the-dots exercise from Chapter 15 in order to find the two or three strongest requirements you can talk about. This will give you the main thrust of your argument.

When opening, start with how you found the position and why it appeals to you. For example:

> *'I am writing to apply for the position of Junior Developer at Amazing Tech Company. When I watched CEO Michelle Lansbury's address to the Java World Congress 2021, I immediately knew I wanted to be part of the ATC team. The products you create are world-changing, and I'd love an opportunity to contribute my expertise in Java and Spring Boot to help your mission of landing the first dog on Neptune. As Ms Lansbury said: "We all need to pull together if we're to push out to the skies."'*

Naturally, if you have permission to refer to a conversation with an actual developer from their team, then you would replace the sentence about the CEO's address with something like:

> *'I recently spoke to Katie Laurence from ATC's development team, who was adamant I should apply. She told me about the culture of excellence and team support, and it sounded like a great fit.'*

Notice that the first paragraph is almost entirely about them, not about you. You want to show that you've done your homework and that you understand their business needs.

The second paragraph should cover your USP and connect it to the company/position. For example:

> *'As a former teacher, I'm not your typical Java developer. I'm a problem-solver and a programmer first, but I will never lose my love of sharing what I learn*

> with others. I pride myself on bringing the whole team with me and lifting up others just as I used to lift up my students. I want to bring those skills to help lift ATC even further, into the skies.'

The next section is where you really bring it home. Take your strongest matches from connect-the-dots and you extrapolate them into text. At this point, it's important to project confidence, so try not to 'qualify' statements. Take the following example:

> 'In the job description, you mention Java is "the cornerstone of our application anatomy". I have been learning Java for two years, including taking courses by Java champion Angie Jones. I may not be an expert yet, but I know the basics and can put together a good API given a bit of time.'

As you can see, the first two sentences are great: they follow the NNQ rule and provide a strong impression. However, the applicant's desire to clarify that they're not an expert suddenly makes the two years sound less impressive. These qualifiers (eg but, however, just, yet) diminish the strong impact of using NNQ.

Let's try again:

> 'In the job description, you mention Java is "the cornerstone of our application anatomy". I have been learning Java for two years, including taking courses by Java champion Angie Jones. I am able to use Java to create REST APIs in Spring Boot, and I have experience working with others via pair programming to solve bigger issues when they arise.'

Now, the statement remains factual, but it's supported with 'additional' language (eg and, also, additionally, furthermore, as well as).

The cover letter is not a place to be humble, so let go of feeling like you need brutal honesty here. If you're not technically proficient enough, you (and they) will find out at a later stage in the interview process. There's no need to rule yourself out before you've even tried!

Once you've made your case, I find it nice to add a short sentence or two about your personality. This allows the reader to also see what kind of person you'd be like to work with. This is a great place to add your three words if you haven't already. For example:

> 'Personality-wise, I'm a contributor. I love talking through issues with my teammates and finding solutions together. My former manager, David Pilker, describes me as "A diligent worker with a heart of gold", and I pride myself on exactly that.'

You should then wrap up with a generic statement thanking them for the opportunity and expressing your hope to hear from them soon.

Last but not least, I want to mention the *super special* jobs. By that, I mean a job you come across that sounds so perfectly suited to you, so absolutely spot-on for your experience and personality, that you would drop every other opportunity for it. If you're lucky enough to find a position like this, then I encourage you to also adapt your LinkedIn profile and your portfolio site or GitHub profile.

For example, when applying for my current position, I knew that DEI (diversity, equity, and inclusion) initiatives were part of the job. I changed my LinkedIn title from 'Software Engineer | Motivational Speaker | JavaScript, React, Kotlin, Spring Boot' to 'Software Engineer | Speaker | Diversity Enthusiast'. I also changed my pinned posts to include a blog post I'd written about supporting women in the workplace and checked all of my work experience descriptions, adding back in some of my media experience.

Had I been applying to more technical jobs at the same time, this change would not necessarily have supported those applications. However, the position fit me so well, and I wasn't actively searching for other jobs anyway, so I adapted everything to highlight what I knew they were looking for.

Remember, throughout this process, you need to think of everything from the recruiter's perspective. They're trying to find a fit that they can sell to the rest of the company or to their boss: help make their job as easy as possible by adapting what you send!

Recruiter Contact

You've now adapted all your documents, but there's still one step left before applying: contacting the recruiter. This step is scary because there's no guidebook (other than this one) for how to go about having this conversation, and it requires putting yourself out on a limb.

In case you didn't know, unfortunately, there exists software that automatically filters out applications without a human ever reading them. This software scans CVs and application documents for keywords (e.g. programming languages, specific skills, or preferred former employers) and delivers an automatic rejection if a certain benchmark isn't reached. Therefore, recruiter contact can make a huge difference between your application getting filtered out by a machine and getting seen.

Of course, if there's no recruiter or hiring manager listed on the job ad, then you can choose to forgo this step or find anyone working in HR at the company and send them a message to ask who would be best to contact.

The simplest way to contact a recruiter is to open with a positive statement, describe the situation, and then ask if you could have a short call to discuss. For example:

> 'Hi Tyler, I've seen the job ad for the Front-end Developer position at BreezeWater Inc. I'm a

JavaScript developer with previous experience as a dam engineer, so it was really exciting to find a position that combines my two worlds. I was wondering if we could set up a five-minute call so I could ask you a few questions about the product and company? Sincerely, Anna'

Most recruiters love short phone or video calls like this: they're the bread and butter of the recruiting world. Recruiters enjoy them because it gives them a first look at your personality and acts a bit like a screening interview. For you, it's a great chance to present yourself and your elevator pitch as well as ask one or two questions about the company. If you're wondering what you could ask, simply try to find issues that are *not* mentioned in the job ad. After all, you've done your research, so you want a chance to show that!

Here are some ideas for questions to ask in a short call:

- Is the work remote, on-site, or hybrid?
- How many days of leave are included?
- What's the salary range for the position?
- Does the company provide a budget for ongoing education or conferences?
- How many people are in the team I'd be on?
- Is this a new position or is it replacing someone who left? If it's the latter, why did they leave?

Of course, there's a chance that the recruiter will say no to a short call and will instead prefer to just have you send your application to them directly or via the official channels. If so, that's fine. It's not ideal, but you tried, and now it's time to move on. Similarly, if you don't hear back from them after two days, then apply via the official channels and let it go.

Application

The last step is to save all your documents as PDFs and then send your application kit.

Sometimes, this is done by attaching your CV and cover letter in an email to the recruiter. If so, pay close attention to how they request it. Often, they'll ask you to use a specific subject line or reference code. Make sure you follow their instructions precisely.

Most of the time, however, you'll be asked to send your application kit via some sort of online portal or form. Again, be sure to read it carefully and adapt your documents if needed. The best types of forms only involve your contact details and then a space to upload documents. The worst type of forms involve filling in all of your work history, education, references, etc. Luckily, there are fewer of these behemoths anymore, but you're likely to stumble across a few. This kind of work is particularly draining and frustrating, but that's all the more reason to try to contact the recruiter in advance. If you know they're interested, then the time spent filling in endless forms is easier to justify.

As an organisational note, it's crucial to save the exact versions of the CV and cover letter (as well as any emails or messages you write) alongside your job notes. Remember, there's a chance that you'll apply to dozens or even hundreds of jobs, and if you're constantly adapting your documents, you'll need to know which exact version you sent for which job so you can mirror those appropriately when you get a phone call.

Chapter 17

Understanding The Classic Job Interview Stages For Tech

By following the guidelines in this book, it's my goal to get you past the first major hurdle in getting a tech job: the callback. Once you get that phone call or email, you enter a new stage of the job search. The employer has your information and they're interested, so now you have to convince them that you're the best choice out of the candidates they have.

The difficulty, of course, is that you don't know what the other candidates bring to the table. This is why there's no point in comparing yourself to any other potential applicant. Different people bring different skills. It could be that you're going for the same position as someone else who has read this book! For that reason, it's crucial that you focus on yourself and your own potential. It's the hiring manager's decision to decide who will fit best in their team and why.

For that reason, it's important to understand how the interview process normally works. Of course, there are some companies that will hire you with only two interviews and some (luckily, rare) cases where it will take as many as eight. In general, though, you can expect there to be three stages.

In this chapter, we'll cover what each interview stage is as well as a few outlier examples that can occur.

Screening Call

The screening call is normally a short, 10- to 20-minute conversation about who you are and why you applied for the job. This call can either happen in a planned way (eg with a calendar invite sent to your email address) or the recruiter will simply call you unannounced.

This latter scenario is exactly why your job notes need to be easily accessible at all times. If the phone rings from an unknown number and you can bring up your documents before answering it, that's ideal. Then you can simply click on the job notes in question as soon as they announce what company they're from.

If you're nervous about phone calls and you prefer video, then the planned screening call is a best-case scenario for you. You can request that it be done via video, and the majority of recruiters will be absolutely fine with that.

If, on the other hand, you prefer voice-only but are sent a video request, that's harder to swing. You will eventually need to show your face, be it in person or on video. For one interview, you could get away with saying you're at a parent's house or on holiday with bad internet and request voice-only. However, I would limit this to just one meeting.

You might think this is unfair, but there are actual stories of nervous applicants paying other people to do their interviews for them (yes, really!) and then starting a job being woefully underprepared. Those situations are a waste of everyone's time, and for obvious reasons, employers want to avoid them. Employers need to make sure that you are who you say you are, so they'll need to see your face. If there's a health condition that makes video calls difficult for you, then I would tell them that up-front and see if they can arrange an alternative (eg some type of formal identification).

A screening interview will usually cover the same ground as your cover letter. The interview is normally carried out by a recruiter, and often, these people don't have a strong technical background. For that reason, you don't have to worry too much about impressing them with your technical knowledge: what they really want to know is if you tick the right boxes and if you sound like someone who's good to work with.

Here are some typical questions I would expect in a screening interview:

- Tell us about yourself
- Why are you applying for this job?
- What do you know about the company?
- Do you have any experience in ___?
- Have you programmed with others before?
- Do you prefer working in a team or alone?
- What are your salary expectations for this job?

As the name suggests, what the recruiter is trying to do is see if there's any major reason why they should screen you out. They'll make note if you have no experience in their tech stack, only give single-word answers, have never worked with other programmers before, or have wildly high salary expectations.

I found screening calls to be straightforward, usually very pleasant, and easy to navigate when I was well-prepared and had the job notes in front of me. Most recruiters are friendly, and if you just talk to them as if you're talking to a normal coworker or a friend-of-a-friend at a dinner party, then you should be able to get through the screening interview fairly well.

If you do get screened out, it's probably due to experience. Remember, in some cases, the recruiter is doing you a favour here! If a job really does require someone more experienced, then filling that role would be extremely painful for you (it's a lot of stress being given a task you can't handle!) and frustrating for the company. In the end, what you're looking for is a match between what you need and what a company wants.

First Interview (Mostly Social)

If you got through the screening call, then congratulations! It's time for your first serious job interview.

Most of the time, the first interview is conducted by one or two people who manage or lead the department or the team you'll be joining. Often, these are people who are (or have been) developers themselves or work extremely closely with the development teams. They know the lingo, and they're going to ask you some questions about your technical proficiency.

However, I would still say that the majority of first interviews are more social in nature. A lot of the questions that arise will be similar to the cover letter contents and the screening call, but you'll be expected to give longer answers and ask more questions in return.

In this interview, the managers or leads are trying to establish two things:

1. Does this person have the basic knowledge I would expect for this position?
2. Can I imagine being in meetings with this person every day of my working life?

Come into these interviews with solid examples of projects you've completed, problems you've solved, and any scenario in which you've worked in a team to develop something. As a reminder, meetups, hackathons, and online communities are great for finding opportunities to gain this experience.

As someone who has conducted many first interviews, I would say the pass rate here is normally 40-50%. The most common problems I've seen are candidates who:

- Answer questions with single words or extremely short sentences
- Give generic answers that could describe anyone
- Don't know anything about the position or the company
- Have no questions to ask about the job at all
- Add so many qualifiers that you're unsure what they really learned or didn't learn
- Can't give concrete examples of anything

By going in prepared—having your elevator pitch and USP ready, knowing what the job requirements are, and having practical examples of how you meet them—you will already be ahead of the broad majority of candidates.

Second Interview (Technical)

The final interview, the technical interview, is a point of massive contention in the tech community. Simply put, there's no straightforward answer on how this is done or how it *should* be done.

The goal of the technical interview, from the employer's perspective, is to determine if you have the skills to do the job they're hiring you for. Traditionally, it was also called a 'whiteboard' interview. A candidate would enter the room (since, remember, all of this was happening on-site) and be introduced to a programming problem. They would then be asked to use a whiteboard to demonstrate how they would go about breaking this problem down and then solving it.

Nowadays, with most technical interviews taking place remotely, the game has changed a bit. There are four technical test methods that I hear about regularly, which you're more likely to face nowadays:

1. <u>Programming challenge sites</u>: Websites such as HackerRank, Edabit, Exercism, and many more provide bite-sized programming challenges. Companies can request you complete one or several of these live in a session with them. This is the closest thing to a whiteboard test, albeit with actual programming involved.

2. <u>The take-home test</u>: The company sends you a brief explaining what you need to create (eg an anagram finder, a terminal programme, a banking website, etc) and then they give you a set time period (usually one to seven days) to complete it, push it to GitHub, and then share your solution with them before a set interview time to discuss your solution.

3. <u>The live codebase test</u>: As part of the technical interview call, you're given some code (eg via a GitHub repository) to pull and run. In the call, you'll be asked to debug some element of the code or to add a new feature.

4. <u>Explain your project</u>: The interviewer will ask you to pick one of your submitted projects and load up the code. They might then ask you to walk them through it, change something about it, or add a new feature they want. The idea is that, by letting you work inside one of your own projects, you can feel more relaxed and the interviewer can focus more on your abilities rather than on just getting you into the right files or line of code.

All of these options have pros and cons, however, the second and third options are starting to gain popularity while the first option is dropping out of favour. Many experienced engineers will simply exit an interview process that requires the use of a programming challenge website. The main reason is that these challenges exist in a vacuum and are extremely dissimilar to the actual life and work of a software engineer, especially if the use of search engines isn't allowed. However, most FAANG companies and similar conglomerates will still default to these as a way to screen out candidates.

Usually, however, a technical interview isn't so much about *what* you code but *how* and *why* you code in that way.

It's a common 'trick' in these challenges to ask for more than can be delivered. For example, in a live codebase test, you might be asked to add 5 new features in 90 minutes. In that situation, the common mistake is to hurry and silently try to code as much as possible to get them all done. Instead, you should pick one feature (to begin with) that you think is the easiest to achieve and then narrate out loud how you're solving it. This gives you a 'quick win' and shows how you think about programming problems. You can then, if you have time, move onto a second problem—perhaps something a bit harder. In addition to narrating your actions, you should also be asking questions, even if they're basic ones like 'Do you know which folder that component is in?' If you need to use a search engine, use it and say why: 'I'm just going to quickly check the syntax for array.sort.'

It's normal to not have the answers to every question asked of you in an interview. Be honest and answer those you know (or *think* you know) with your best guess. However, if you don't know the answer and it sounds totally foreign to you, then it's 100% OK to respond with 'Sorry, but I'm not familiar with that concept' It's normal for software engineers to have knowledge gaps, and any interviewer worth their salt will know that.

Naturally, if you can't solve any problems or deliver *any* features that they ask for, you're unlikely to be successful in this round. However, focus on what you can achieve, explain why you're solving it, and keep as calm as possible. Again, the interviewers aren't purely assessing your technical skills: they want to see if you'd be good to work with.

Sometimes, there will be multiple technical rounds, but most companies and hiring managers already know how stressful technical interviews can be. As such, they will often avoid putting you through them unnecessarily. If they do, it's usually because there's some tough competition, and they need to distinguish between your skills and that of another candidate. Focus on yourself and your reasoning, and ask lots of questions to show you're a team player.

Other Types Of Interviews That Can Occur

If you're successful in the technical interview and provide a better all-around impression than any other candidate at that stage, then you will, most likely, be offered the job.

However, some companies add extra stages to their interview process. This is particularly true for FAANG because of the extremely high volume of applicants they process. Other larger companies might add extra stages too.

Here are the three most common 'extra steps' I've seen in the industry:

1. <u>Abstract challenge:</u> These challenges involve hypothetical questions that sound like they have a single answer. However, it's more about testing how you break down a logical problem. Some examples include: 'How many golf balls fit in an aeroplane?', 'How much money would you need to clean all the windows in Berlin?', or 'What type of furniture could I make with wood from the tree in front of my house?'. These challenges are also starting to fall out of favour.

2. Team picking: In this interview, you talk to several team leads or the teams themselves to see who would want you to join them. Usually, this is an extremely good sign: it means the company wants to hire you, but they just want to find where you'll be most impactful. For those of us who weren't good at high-school sports, it may bring back some painful memories, but just remember that, if you're in this team picking, you've already hit the big leagues.

3. Chat with the boss: Although it's less likely for a junior position, smaller companies and startups will sometimes bring the CEO or managing director in at the end of the interview process. Usually, this is because the technical staff are happy with you, but the CEO/MD still wants the final say and to be familiar with everyone entering their company. Relax, smile, and remember that this chat is almost entirely about showing you'd be a good colleague.

All of these extra interviews are a good sign of your progress through the application process. If they go well, you can be very hopeful about your chances of getting a contract!

Chapter 18

Interview Preparation

As you can see, each interview stage comes with its own challenges, but the core principle remains the same: know your pitch, know what makes you unique, and then connect it all to what the job is and the employer offering it.

In this chapter, we'll look specifically at preparing for technical tests before moving on to overall preparation techniques and then end on preparing for four of the most common interview questions you're likely to face.

In addition to common interview questions, there are also many common preparation techniques that can apply to multiple stages of the interview process. For example, you should always review the job notes and the company website before any interview. Get yourself into that job's particular mindset, try to imagine what the interviewer is looking for, and focus on one or two key points you really want to communicate.

For example, when interviewing for my current position, I went into the final interview with three points I wanted to communicate:

1. <u>For diversity</u>: Being on the women's advocacy core team at my software engineering job

2. <u>For teamwork</u>: The workshop I was preparing to help technical staff learn stage confidence

3. <u>For community work</u>: The two to three meetups I would speak at in the coming months.

I managed to get points two and three across during the interview and considered that a strong result.

Naturally, there are many other preparation techniques you can use for technical and non-technical interviews. As always, feel free to pick and choose from my recommendations below. Unless you have a lot of time, you're unlikely to be able to use all of them. However, the goal is to give you a range of tools and options so that you can pick from them as you see fit and target any areas that need strengthening. With that said, this chapter has a lot of ground to cover, so let's jump straight in!

Technical Preparation

Technical tests can take many different forms, and it can be hard to know in advance what type you will face. If it were up to me, every company would include an overview of the interview stages in the job description so as to save time, effort, and stress. However, given that we know what the usual types of tests look like, there's some level of general technical preparation that can be done to help improve your chances.

It would be remiss of me to jump into this section without mentioning *the* book on technical interview preparation, which you will (rightly) see mentioned everywhere: *Cracking the Coding Interview* by Gayle Laakmann McDowell. McDowell has worked for three of the five FAANG companies and has been on Google's hiring committee. If you continue to be rejected at the technical stage or recognise technical tests as a particular pain point for you, then I highly recommend reading it.

Furthermore, the traditional coding challenge test usually highlights a concept called 'data structures and algorithms'. Since this isn't a technical manual, I won't go into too much detail about what these are and why they're important, but the basic idea is that it revolves around concepts and strategies for solving common coding problems as efficiently as possible. Being familiar with these and being able to apply them is a great asset to your technical learning but not necessary for the day-to-day work of a junior developer. However, knowing these puts you at a distinct advantage, and if you're applying to FAANG or similar companies, you'll want to add this to your learning as soon as possible.

Flashcards are an age-old way to help memorise certain concepts and can certainly be used for learning both general coding concepts (eg single-responsibility principle, variable declaration vs initialisation, class inheritance, etc) and data structures and algorithms. Nowadays, there are a plethora of flashcard applications and websites you can use for this purpose. You might find existing databases of concepts you can apply, however, I'd encourage you to manually create each flashcard yourself. Remember recall vs recognition from Chapter 1? Writing the cards yourself helps you trigger your 'recall' muscles. Similarly, when using these flashcards, try to speak your answers out loud rather than just thinking about them. This will help prepare you for answering an interviewer if they ask you to define hoisting, for example.

As I mentioned in Chapter 16, however, the technical interviews aren't always about pure technical skill or memorisation. Most of the time, they want to see that you can *communicate* about code. You can explain what you're doing and why and write code that's readable for a human. In short, they want to see that you're skilled at developing code with and for a team rather than just any code that works.

For coding challenges, most of the same websites used by employers are also accessible by everyday developers. Search them out, start with basic/beginner questions, and then work your way through. To train your communication muscles, make it a habit to narrate what you're doing as you practice. Here's an example for a simple JavaScript exercise. The following could be said while typing or before/after typing each part:

> 'So, the exercise asks us to create a function that adds two numbers together. The first thing I'm going to do is create a function, and I'll call it "addNums". I'm going to give it two parameters, "numA" and "numB", and then open the function parentheses. Inside, I'm going to return a number that's "numA" plus "numB". Let's see if that works, and if it does, then we can start adding some type controls to make sure nobody enters a string or something.'

If you don't have much practice at talking about code, this could take you a while to master. Simply put, it can be hard to think about a problem, code a solution, and speak at the same time. Take as many pauses as you like, but again, *practice by speaking out loud*. If you're worried about what your friends, housemates, or family might think, just let them know in advance what's going on!

There is, of course, one final, great way to prepare for any type of technical interview: pair programming. I mentioned in Section 2 that having a good network isn't just about getting job leads and that being sociable will help your actual programming skill. Pair programming is just one example of that. In pair programming, one person 'drives' (does the typing, clicking, etc) and the other person 'navigates' (explains where to go and what's going to change). The actual code that's written, however, is usually collaborative.

Ideally, a technical interview tha's in a codebase (ie not a coding challenge/exercise) should feel very much like pair programming. If you can find one or more developers in your community who are willing to spend even half an hour with you while you work on one of your projects, then you will have a great basis for practising these skills. Again, explain what you're doing, what you're looking for, or how you plan to solve something. Involve them, ask for clarification, or get their opinions on any questions that come up. Remember, good pair programming sessions are collaborative. You're not expected to know everything!

A combination of flashcards, exercises, and pair programming will prepare you well for a technical interview. If it seems like too much, you can always choose just one or two of these things to get started, especially if you already feel confident in your technical ability. Of course, if you want to go further, there's always room to grow, for example, through online courses and video tutorials. Keep recall vs recognition in mind though, and remember that practice is the cornerstone of mastery.

Physical and Mental Preparation

Interviewing makes people nervous. So nervous that some people shut down. So nervous that some people can't stop talking. It's an entire skill unto itself, and one that most people don't have to do particularly often, so there aren't many chances to become desensitised to the nerves. Therefore, it's absolutely crucial that you prepare and practice in advance. Not because it lessens your nervousness, but because it means that you can reduce unknown or unstable elements and reach the point of muscle memory in taking care of the hardest parts.

When I was an opera singer, dealing with stage fright was a huge topic. The energy from nervous performers backstage was palpable and part of what made any production so exciting and fun to be part of. However, there exists a fine line between using nervousness for energy and being consumed by nerves.

I'm going to offer you a piece of advice that was offered to me when I was completing my masters degree in opera performance. Rather than trying to deny that you feel nervous, instead *recognise* your nerves and prepare coping mechanisms in advance.

For example, rather than thinking, 'OK, this is fine. I'll be fine. There's no need to feel nervous. Just shake it off!' try something more like 'I'm feeling nervous right now, and I know when I'm nervous that my hands get a bit shaky. If I notice that happening, I'm going to clasp my hands together on my lap or behind my back.' Some other techniques I've seen used are:

- <u>For freezing up</u>: Take a slow sip of water to give yourself time to think.

- <u>For panic</u>: Focus on taking a breath between each sentence.

- <u>For overtalking</u>: Wrap up a sentence with a key phrase, for example 'You get the idea' or 'That sort of thing'.

In each case, the idea isn't to try to stop the nerves or the physical symptoms of the nerves but to find a coping strategy to adapt.

Of course, this can be hard to prepare for if you don't know what you do when you're nervous. Perhaps you haven't been in this kind of environment before or in a long time, and you don't know how you'll react. This is one of many reasons why, more likely than not, your first interview will not be successful. The good news is that, like any failure, you can learn from it. Once you know how you physically react to stress, you can come up with coping mechanisms to get you through.

On-Site Interviews

Let's take a moment to cover how to prepare for on-site interviews. More and more interviews happen online now; however, it's not uncommon for a company to want to complete one of the interview stages in an office or a live environment. Doing so provides some benefits, but it also provides several challenges.

Let's begin with something that's so often overlooked: what you wear. In terms of dress code, tech is one of the few industries where you can wear almost anything to a job interview. Nevertheless, I would still recommend dressing business casual for an interview and not just wearing your favourite jeans-and-hoodie combo.

That said, regardless of *what* you wear, the bigger issue is *how* you wear it. Many people like to pick out a new or impressive outfit for an interview but forget to practice in it. For example, you might wear a new blouse and pants that look great when you're standing looking in the mirror. But are you able to move enough in them to complete a whiteboard interview? If you lift your arms up, will your belly show? If you sit down, will the shirt ride up and show your underwear? If you're wearing new shoes, especially heels, can you walk comfortably up stairs in them? What about on carpet? It's worth trying on the *entire* outfit (including any special hair, makeup, or jewellery) and practising your interview while wearing it.

Now that you're dressed, the next thing to practice is walking into the room. As a stage performer who had to perform countless auditions, I was often told, 'Don't rule yourself out before you've even opened your mouth.' You would be surprised how many people slouch, walk slowly into a room, never smile, or appear generally hesitant about being there. Undoubtedly, much of this has to do with nerves or general comfort around other people; however, the best thing you can do is to try to give a strong first impression. Enter the room with the best posture you have (shoulders back, chest out, eyes up), flash your interviewer your best smile, open with a 'Pleasure to meet you', and extend a handshake (if appropriate). Similarly, you can also practise standing up from a chair, saying 'Thank you for your time, it was a pleasure meeting you' and walking out.

The best way to practise is with a camera. Spoiler alert: this won't be the last time I recommend you film yourself! Most people despise seeing and hearing recordings of themselves. Your voice always sounds higher than you think it is, and it can be hard to reconcile the person you see with the way you internally view yourself. However, there are so many things about ourselves that we just can't notice using a mirror.

Friends or family can be very helpful but also tend to sugarcoat their feedback. In short, nothing replaces actually watching yourself, taking note of one or two things you want to improve, and then repeating the process.

Lastly, I want to give you a quick tip for jogging your brain in a live interview. When attending a live interview, you should bring a small folder with two copies of your CV and, potentially, also a page with some questions written on it. Bring water with you, or if they offer you water, accept it. At the start of the interview, you can remove a copy of your CV and offer it to the interviewer. They will likely already have one, so you can then leave your copy in front of you. If you get stuck on a question, this allows you to take a sip of water and use the process of drinking as an opportunity to take a look at your CV's motivation statement. Although it shouldn't be anything new to you (after all, you'll have reviewed that motivation statement, your job notes, and your cover letter *many* times by this point), it will hopefully be able to steer you back to a talking point that you can use in some way.

Video Interviews

In my opinion, there isn't much of a difference between a live interview and a video interview. The main difference is the technical setup and how much you can get away with in terms of nerves.

For one thing, nervous ticks, heavy breathing, or shaking are far less visible on video than in-person, so your coping mechanisms don't have to be as thorough. You can twiddle your thumbs or squeeze a stress ball off-camera and nobody will ever be the wiser!

The other major benefit is that you can use notes during the interview more openly. I mentioned that having a page of questions is fine to bring into a live interview, and of course, you can also jot down the answers to those questions to take with you if you want. However, in an online interview, you can have notes or short prompts ready to answer some of the common questions we'll cover soon. I often use the notes to write down the names and job titles of everyone in the interview or one or two key talking points in case that information becomes relevant. When asked for questions, I'll openly say, 'Let me have a look at my notes' and then scan my prepared questions for one that hasn't already been answered during the interview. Simply put: I never deny that I have or use notes, and nobody ever seems to mind!

Despite these benefits, there's still some preparation and practice required for online interviews. For one thing, you should have a camera set up in a position that clearly shows your face, ideally at eye level or higher. Additionally, you should ensure that there will be enough light on your face, especially if the interview takes place at night. If there isn't enough light, use a lamp or ring light. If you wear makeup, also remember that these kinds of lights will wash out the colour in your face, so you might need to apply it with a heavier hand than usual.

Of course, the best way to determine all of this is to practice! Again, wear the exact outfit, hairstyle, makeup, jewellery, etc that you're planning to wear for the interview itself, and record yourself answering practice questions while looking into the camera.

It's common for people on camera to watch the other participants while talking in a group call, but I encourage you to try looking directly into the lens of your webcam instead. At first, this will feel very odd because you're staring at a piece of hardware rather than anyone's eyes or face. How can you read their reactions? It's impossible. However, much more important than you seeing their exact facial expressions is them seeing your eyes. Explaining something directly to the camera helps the viewers feel closer to you, and they will see you as more honest because of it.

Practising Common Interview Questions

When you record yourself practising for your interviews, be sure to not only evaluate how well you answered the question but also how well you engage the viewer by speaking in a way that shows enthusiasm. If you feel like you become flat or monotone at any point, try to work out why and how you could put more energy into it. This is a tiring, repetitive process. However, it works.

By practising consistently, not only will you learn what habits of yours are effective and ineffective, but you'll also learn your answers for common questions. If you're singing karaoke in your car, how confidently do you sing a new song vs a classic from your childhood? Learning the words and repeating them enables you to focus on delivery. This is another classic principle direct from the stage: 'The true work begins once the script is memorised.'

Although I don't recommend rote learning for your answers, I do recommend coming up with two to three bullet points for answering each one and memorising those. Once you have them memorised, your practice can begin to focus on flow, eliminating qualifiers (as a reminder, those are words like 'but',''however', 'only', and 'just'), and fluidly connecting ideas.

With that said, let's have a quick look at five of the most common interview questions and what kinds of answers you should be giving.

'Tell Us About Yourself'

This question is, simply put, an open invitation to drop in your standard 'About Me' description you developed during your branding exercises. Combine your USP and your brand words to give a quick summary (three to four sentences) of your background and experience as it's relevant to the particular position.

Unlike your standard elevator pitch, this pitch needs to be specific to the role for which you're applying. Again, put yourself in the shoes of the interviewer and think about what they're looking for. Tailor your answer to that need!

'Why Do You Want To Work Here?'

You can think of this question as a test of you having done your homework. Although it's true that the main reason people want to work anywhere is, well, to have a job and earn money, it's also true that employers want to find employees who will show them a certain level of loyalty and dedication. Employers know that 'purpose' is part of what makes people stay in a job, so they want to see if your purpose aligns with what they're offering since that will make you more likely to stay in the job for longer.

When formulating your answer to this question, review the job notes and/or the company website and remind yourself of their mission. What are they trying to achieve on a macro level? What do they, therefore, need on an individual or team level?

Open with their needs and their mission and then connect it with your experience and areas of interest. Again, this is a restatement of your cover letter, but it should be phrased in a way that's related to what the employer needs. If you can, show visible excitement about what the company does, actually call it 'cool' or 'exciting', and end by highlighting the idea that you have a lot to offer and would be excited to contribute.

'What Are Your Strengths And Weaknesses?'

This question isn't so in fashion at the moment, but it still pops up often enough to warrant a discussion. It's also a question that a lot of applicants don't maximise on.

The most common mistake here is to answer with too little information: 'Well, I'd say my strength is that I'm focused and a good team player. My weaknesses would be that I'm sometimes too detail-oriented, so I get distracted from the bigger picture.'

What the above quote is missing are examples.

For strengths, you should give examples of times when those strengths helped a project, team, or job you completed. Remember NNQ: for example, for being a good team player, you could refer to the number of people you worked with or reference a quote or compliment from a named coworker. Here's an example from one of my interviews: 'I'd say my biggest strength is that I'm a good team player. When I worked in opera, we would have to coordinate 50 or 60 people on a stage, and to do that effectively, you need to be able to truly trust everyone on the team and reliably do your part.'

For weaknesses, you should explain how that weakness has impacted you in the past and what you try to do to counter it. For example: 'My biggest weakness would be that I'm very detail-oriented. In the past, that's meant that I've gone down rabbit holes about clean code instead of actually programming. I've been trying to counter that by giving myself dedicated research time for deeper concepts so that I can use my programming time to focus directly on the task at hand.'

Yes, this takes up a lot of words, but it becomes clear to the interviewer that you're being honest (ie this is a real weakness and not 'I'm just too much of a perfectionist' or similar) and that you're actively looking for strategies to improve on your weaknesses.

'What Is Your Expected Salary For This Position?'

This question is the bane of everyone's existence, especially for positions that haven't listed any salary range in their job ads. There are really only three strategies for dealing with this question:

1. Put the question back on them: This is what most professional career coaches recommend. Something along the lines of 'What is the range for this position?' or 'What would you expect to pay for

someone of my experience?' are two phrases you can use to turn the question back around.

2. <u>Delay the question until a later stage:</u> This technique requires a bit more confidence, but it also requires being willing to potentially waste your time on a job that could pay less than you want or need. An example would be to say, 'If you find me to be a suitable candidate, then you can make me an offer at the end of the interview process, and we can evaluate from there.'

3. <u>Give an answer:</u> Use websites like Glassdoor (or similar regional variants) to look up average salaries for junior developers in your area or at the company. Personally, I always *wanted* to put the question back on them as recommended, but I always ended up chickening out and giving a number. If you're similar, then my advice is to use your research, pick an amount you think sounds appropriate, and then add 10-15% onto it. If you're lucky, they'll say yes to the amount you list. If they give you a counter-offer, then they'll likely go down to the amount you'd have been happy with anyway.

Overall though, try to remember that this question is far more awkward for you than it is for them. That's purely because recruiters in particular have this conversation dozens of times every week, whereas for you, it's a rare occurrence. Simply put, they have more practice talking about salaries.

'What Questions Do You Have For Us?'

I've never heard of any interview that doesn't end with this question. Sometimes, an interview will even open with this question! As such, it's important to have up to five questions prepared in advance. Normally, I would recommend only asking three of them, however, you'll often find that some of your questions are answered during the course of the interview anyway.

It is, however, *absolutely crucial* that you ask something. Do not, under any circumstances, leave an interview without having asked a question.

The main reason for this is power imbalance: you'll seem desperate for a job if you're willing to accept anything with no questions or provisons. Even if you truly are desperate for a job, desperation doesn't usually lend the best impression or lead people to want to work with you.

But an even worse impression is possible: that of not caring at all. If you're seriously considering this job, it's going to impact what you spend a huge part of your day doing. It might impact where you live, how much you can support yourself and your family, and (in the case of the US) it could also impact where you can get medical treatment.

Look up some common questions to ask employers or think about your own life circumstances. Be sure to consider income, benefits, location (remote/on-site/hybrid), flexibility, workplace culture, mentorship/learning opportunities, and how they would plan to onboard you. All of this should be crystal clear to you by the end of the interview process.

Your first tech job could very well impact the course of the rest of your life. Treat an interview less like a grilling and more like a business meeting. You have needs: can the employer meet them? The employer has needs: can you meet them? Ask the questions required to establish these facts.

Chapter 19

After the Interview

When an interview at any stage of the process is over, a huge range of emotions will be swirling around. If things clearly went well, it'll feel similar to a good first date, full of hope and excitement but also nerves. Did they like me as much as I liked them? Did it really go well, or was I just imagining it?

If an interview didn't go well, there are even more emotions flying around: it might trigger feelings of inadequacy, fear of failure, or imposter syndrome. Despite that, there will always be a small part of you that hopes you were wrong. Maybe you didn't really bomb the interview, maybe you're just being hard on yourself. This definitely happens sometimes, but only you and your interviewer can know if that's true or not.

There's one other scenario: you don't want the job anymore. Maybe they mentioned some awful working conditions, maybe it would require you to move out of state or internationally, or maybe they want you to work with a programming language you have no interest in. Regardless of the reason, there's absolutely no problem with either telling them directly in the interview or sending them a follow-up email/message within a few days. I'll say this though, don't continue the interview process if you know you won't accept the job. Just as you wouldn't want your time wasted by an employer who'll never offer you a contract, so too should you extend the same courtesy.

If you do still want the job, there's unlikely to be a follow-up from the recruiter on the same day or even the next day. Most of the time, employers interview multiple people over the course of a week (or two) and it can take a while until you get feedback. In that time, you might also be doing more interviews. Again, this is why the importance of a tracking document can't be overstated.

In general, one of the questions you can always ask in an interview is 'What are the next steps?' or 'When will I hear from you about the next steps?' This signals to the interviewer that you want to continue the process (showing enthusiasm is always good!), but it mainly allows you to set expectations. For some employers, a two to three week feedback period isn't uncommon. However, if you don't know that, then you might begin to give up hope after two to three days.

Should I Send a Follow-Up Message?

If you didn't ask the question, and they haven't given you any indication about the waiting period, then it's 100% fine to send the recruiter a quick email or LinkedIn message a week after your interview. For example:

> *'Hi Frank,*
>
> *Thank you again for arranging the interview last week—it was great to meet you. As it's been a week now, I wanted to quickly check in and see if there's any news about the progress of my application. Any updates would be greatly appreciated: as you can imagine, I'm interviewing with several companies right now, so my schedule is getting a bit tight!'*

The last sentence is optional, but the great thing about a follow-up like this is that, regardless of whether they liked you or not, they'll feel more inclined to give you an answer. If they didn't like you, then knowing about your other applications will remove some guilt for them (they are human, after all) and allow them to more openly reject you. If they like you, they'll feel the pressure of competition and start fighting to keep you in their process. Either way, you win.

You might be thinking 'Hang on, how do I win from them rejecting me?' Simply put, you shouldn't waste time or energy on a job you won't get. If they've already decided that you're not one of their top candidates, then you won't get that job. Spending time or, more importantly, emotional energy (ie hope, not knowing the result, stress) on a job you'll never get is a waste of your resources. In short, receiving a rejection is a far better outcome than never receiving an answer at all.

Furthermore, a rejection gives you space to ask for feedback. Unfortunately, recruiter feedback is rarely particularly useful; however, occasionally, you'll receive feedback from a technical member of the staff who can actually tell you why you were screened out and that can, in turn, help you know what to focus on for the next interview.

Dealing with Rejection

More often than not, the interview process will end in a rejection. There's no sugar-coating it. It sucks.

I believe that a large part of why so many applicants default to a 'spray and pray' approach to job applications is to save them time and effort but also in part to deflect some of the pain that comes from a rejection for a job for which you spent so much time preparing.

I haven't written much about my operatic background regarding its intersection with tech, but it's worth mentioning here because it prepared me for rejection in a way that I feel uniquely qualified to talk about it. If you've ever created an artwork, written a poem, or made something truly from the heart, then I want you to imagine handing that over to someone whose opinion you value and then having them take a brief, disinterested look at it before tearing it up and throwing it in the bin. That's what an opera audition feels like.

Opera singers work tirelessly at their craft, from music theory to vowel differentiation, from emotional expression to acting, from the international phonetic alphabet to breathing. Then they apply it methodically to a new piece of music and practice it countless times before presenting it to an audition panel. About 99% of the time, that panel will show very little interest or simply list all the things they didn't like straight to the singer's face. In one singing competition, the jury spent 10 minutes explaining everything they thought I was doing wrong before ending with 'But at least you look great!' Ouch.

In comparison, tech interviews are relatively mild. In fact, the most frustrating part of rejection in the tech world is getting so little feedback that you can be left absolutely flummoxed. 'I thought I did well but still didn't get the job', you think. 'What aren't I seeing?'

Allow me to be blunt: what you're not seeing are the other candidates. Perhaps the winning candidate has more freelance experience, worked at the company in a different role and is known to be a great colleague, or offered a particularly good technical insight during the test. There are any number of reasons why another candidate would be chosen over you. That doesn't change your value, it just means that in this particular instance, you were unlucky.

The 'One Step Closer' Concept

Rejection also means that you are now one step closer to the job where *you* are considered the perfect candidate. A position where those hiring you are thrilled to give you the call, excited to welcome you onto the team, and excited to invest time and money into your development. That job is out there, but this wasn't it.

The broad majority of new developers will apply to dozens, or potentially hundreds, of jobs before getting an offer. By viewing each rejection as 'one step closer', you can take each interview as a learning opportunity. Practice really does get you to Carnegie Hall, so view your applications and interviews in particular as practice for when the real deal comes along.

Even after all that, there's no denying that rejection will hurt, especially early on in your search and for positions you feel uniquely suited for. Allow yourself to feel that emotion. Vent to your friends, partner, family, or online community about it. One method I've heard of is to allow yourself five minutes to feel sorry for yourself, swear, hit a pillow, scream into the void, or do whatever you want. After five minutes, move on. The idea is that it's important to express your emotions but just as important not to wallow in them.

Lifelong Roommate

Another concept I use to help myself in times of failure is to remember that we have one person who's our roommate for our entire lives: ourselves. A roommate is a great resource: we can vent to them, talk about our successes, get annoyed at them when they don't do chores, and relax with them on the couch. Similarly, you should treat yourself as you would treat a roommate or a best friend.

Imagine your roommate comes home and says, 'I failed an interview. I'm pathetic. I'm ignorant. I shouldn't have ever thought I could do this job.' How would you react? I'm guessing you would reassure them and tell them it's only one interview and there are plenty more fish in the sea, etc.

I like to use this concept to adjust how I talk to myself in moments of failure. Rather than letting the negative, self-deprecating side 'win', I imagine that my subconscious is just my roommate. Learning to engage in positive, encouraging self-talk can be a crucial way to reevaluate what you're feeling and extend yourself some kindness.

Motivation Hits and Becoming Resilient

By far the hardest part of rejection is the hit it delivers to your motivation. If you're lucky, you're the kind of person who fights harder the more you feel like something is impossible. Most people aren't like this, however, and get a bit down on themselves.

Early on in the application process, say for the first 10-20 applications you send, it's easy to follow my advice and stay positive. What about after 50 applications? What about after 100 applications?

I *hope* that by following the advice in this book, and applying it rigorously, you won't have to engage in hundreds of applications. The truth is though, that I don't know the market you're operating in, and I can't guarantee anything. But my general advice remains, '*keep going*'.

Motivation is very difficult to manufacture. What I can say is this: You belong in tech regardless of your background, your race, your gender identity, your sexuality, your religion, your native language, or your mental health condition. If you can apply yourself enough to read this book, follow its advice, and learn a programming language, then you can get a job in tech.

The best advice I can give you when your motivation wanes is to just *show up*. Sit back down at the computer, open your IDE, and get coding—even if that means only 30 minutes every day. Show up to events, keep meeting people, and try to stay positive about your prospects. Send a job application once a week or once every two weeks if that's all you can handle. Show up to the interviews. Be there.

Resilience is one of the best traits you can have, and it's a skill like any other. You're trying to change your life: it's going to take time and it's going to be hard. If it weren't difficult, then everyone would have a tech job within a month of creating a 'Hello, world' application. Keep showing up and try to get through it. You've come too far to stop.

Resilience doesn't mean 'hustle culture'. That is, you shouldn't be pushing yourself to think about tech or do coding exercises all day, every day. You shouldn't be sacrificing your mental health just to complete flashcards. Resilience means taking stock of what you can handle, even if that's just five minutes a day or two hours a week, and maintaining some sort of forward motion in your learning, even in the face of disappointment or failure.

Taking a Break from the Job Search

Showing up is a huge part of success, but there comes a time when you might need to acknowledge that you weren't ready for the job search after all. This is the situation when taking a break is appropriate.

Even then, 'taking a break' isn't taking a break from tech in total. You should reevaluate what you've learned and what's been asked of you in interviews. You should revisit your communities, chat with your network about how the interviews have gone, and see if there's anyone who can give advice on your weak points. Furthermore, you should revisit your learning plan and your branding kit and either revise them or start new ones.

Of course, you *can* take a total break from tech. In cases of burnout or mental anguish, I don't recommend pushing and pushing and pushing. Sometimes, the best thing you can do is get some distance, spend some time with the people you love, get some exercise, and look at some green things. Personally, this approach often helps me to reconfigure my priorities and keep things in perspective. Usually, doing this also helps remind you of why you wanted to pursue a tech career in the first place.

Should I Quit Trying to be a Developer?

I'm going to state this as simply and directly as I can: Rejection is not a good reason to quit.

Rejection, and failure of any kind, is a learning opportunity. It allows you to evaluate how you can improve, create a plan for that improvement, and then achieve results. Every tiny improvement you make gets you closer to the success you're looking for, regardless of what success looks like for you. If you have this attitude, you maintain it, and you really want this career, then you shouldn't quit.

I wouldn't have written this book if I didn't believe that it would help you get a job in tech. I don't know how many applications you've submitted, how many blog posts you've written, or how many contacts you've made. I can't control how many jobs are available in your area, any biases the interview panel might have, or how nervous you get when you sit down for a technical interview. All I know and all I can give you, I've shared in this book.

If, however, you've come to the conclusion that you cannot apply for another single job, but you know you're job-ready, and you're so frustrated that you could scream and throw in the towel, then I will give you one final piece of advice: Freelance.

I have already written about the pros and cons of freelancing in a previous chapter; however, the biggest advantage is that it allows you to earn money while gaining experience. Most of the time, if you take freelancing seriously (ie you're not making a terrible website for $20), and you treat it as your new career, then it might be a big leap of faith, but it will allow you to continue the forward motion I mentioned regarding resilience.

With that said, there are a few legitimate reasons to quit tech completely:

1. You've found another career that you think will be more fulfilling.

2. Your current job has given you some sort of promotion or opportunity that will bring you the joy and/or income you wanted from tech.

3. There's been a change in your circumstances and changing careers would severely impact your quality of life.

4. You decide that it's no longer high enough of a priority to dedicate time to.

5. You've experienced some sort of trauma connected to tech that you can't move past.

Notice that I didn't say anything about programming being too hard or you losing interest in it. That's because tech is an *enormous* field, and there are so many other jobs you can pursue if you decide that programming isn't what you want to do in tech. Leads, recruiters, scrum masters, product owners, advocates, etc are all positions in high demand. You can still contribute! Revisit Chapter 5 to read more about these jobs and then it might be time to pivot.

Overall though, you're likely to just be reading this section while feeling a bit down about the job search, so I encourage you to keep going. Be kind to yourself.

Final Contact

When you receive a rejection email, it can be tempting to just swear loudly, slam the laptop shut, and walk away. Even if this is indeed your first reaction, I would always recommend emailing them back once you're calm to thank them for their time and request any specific feedback they can give about what would have made your application stronger. If you're rejected by phone, then it's worth doing the same thing verbally *before the call ends*. It's much easier to get an answer when you're on the phone than via email, and you can always write down the feedback in your tracking document.

Most employers do not give valuable feedback, but some do. Even if what they send or say to you isn't particularly useful, it's still polite to thank them and show that you're trying to improve. For all you know, you were their second or third choice, and this little nicety could be part of what gets you a call for the next position they open.

Dealing with an Offer

Congratulations! You got an offer!

If this is your first offer, you might be tempted to immediately say yes and jump into a contract signing. However, I'd advise you to first consider a few questions before you even agree verbally to a position:

1. Do you have any other job interviews that are close to the final stages that you would prefer?
2. Are the conditions really something you can live with for a year or more?

The first question is about risk vs reward. Is the risk of losing this offer worth it for the reward of getting the job you would *love*? Only you can answer that question. The earlier you are in the application process, the more risk you can take on here. Having an offer on your second or third application (wow!) means you've done a great job and are probably considered a good team asset. That means the risk of not getting any other offers is low. If, however, you've passed a few dozen applications and this is your first offer, you will have to truly weigh how likely you are to get offered the other job.

If you're brave enough, one direct way to check this is to literally call or email the recruiter for the job you love and tell them directly that you have another offer. For example:

> '*I wanted to inform you that I've been made an offer for a junior developer position at Glorious Tech Company. However, I am so excited about my application with you for this job. If I am considered a frontrunner, and if you can move the final interview up a few days, that would be a best-case scenario. If that's not possible, or if the feeling is that I am unlikely to be the #1 choice, then please let me know so I can accept this offer.*'

As I mentioned earlier, most employers want someone excited about and dedicated to their job. If a recruiter knows that you would reject another position to take this one, that can look very good. Furthermore, they know that recruiting is a business. You are valuable, and if they know someone else wants you, that might actually increase your chances of going the distance. Overall, sending a message such as this one comes with very few risks but makes sure everyone is on the same page. It can also potentially release you from the 'What if...' question you would otherwise be asking yourself.

In terms of the second question, I would advise you to never take a position you can't imagine holding for a year. The reason for this is simple: once you have one year of professional experience on your CV, the recruiters will come to you. The demand for mid- and senior-level developers is huge, so having a year or more of experience basically puts you in a completely different category than a junior. If this is your strategy, then I recommend you continue blogging and staying active on social media and in your communities. That could mean the difference between a small income increase vs a massive one.

Another consideration could be that the salary offered is too low. Hopefully, the offered amount shouldn't be too surprising to you, as you've talked to the recruiter about it before this. If you want to negotiate, I again ask you to consider risk vs reward. If you're feeling confident about your job search, and feel strongly that you can get a better offer, say that. Say that you'll only accept X amount and see how they react. Again, it might feel awkward for you, but for recruiters, this is standard business. You're unlikely to shock them unless you ask for something totally unreasonable for your level and region. If you want a guideline, I wouldn't ask for 10-15% more than whatever they offer you.

On the flip side, if you've been struggling to find work, I would err on the side of accepting the offer. It might not be sexy advice to take a low-salary offer, however, if you can perform well in your first year, then you have the option of either asking for a significant raise or switching jobs and getting a significant raise. Either way, securing that first year of experience could be worth the low starting salary.

If none of these scenarios are a problem for you and you're satisfied with the conditions offered (at least for a year!), go ahead and sign. Remember, though, nothing is guaranteed until the contract is signed! Do not consider your job search over or cancel any other interviews until that moment comes to pass.

Once all the parties have signed: Congratulations! You've made it into tech!

Key Takeaways

The first job is the hardest to find. It will take time, effort, and patience. You'll need to rely not only on your branding kit and your technical skills but also on your network. You'll need to talk to people far more than you may have thought: local developers, recruiters, hiring managers, and anyone who can practise with you.

In this section, you learned how to prepare all the most important documents to apply for a programming job as well as how to adapt those depending on the job. Tracking your applications and keeping notes about each company and their job offers forms the cornerstone of this highly analytical approach. It's not just about staying organised, it's about approaching the job search as a learning process, just like you did as you learned to code.

Hopefully, this section enabled you to search out positions at companies you may not have considered or see how the domain knowledge you gained from a former career can act as a significant boost to your job search rather than a hindrance or a question mark. The skills and abilities you bring to a job are multifaceted, especially if you're coming from another career or are an older applicant.

Searching for a job is a skill like any other: it takes practice and honest self-reflection. Each rejection is like a new scrum sprint retrospective: look at where things went wrong, take notes, learn from it, and do better the next time. Slowly, you will become more practised at interviews, and by seeing each rejection as being *one step closer* to the real job, you'll hopefully be able to maintain your motivation and your positivity.

If not, you risk becoming a low-energy candidate, spamming CVs to any job listed, not really knowing which interview you're going into, and seeing every rejection as a personal insult. Do not allow yourself to get caught in that cycle. Treat every single application as its own micro experiment, testing out your branding kit, your application kit, and your ability to pitch yourself. As with any experiment, you have to keep learning from it because it can take dozens or even hundreds of attempts before you find the right job with which you can get started in this industry.

Another huge takeaway from this section is the benefit of preparation and practice. As a former opera singer, I know the value of these things. Just as I did scales every day, so too should you be practising your pitch, learning how to connect the dots of your experience with the requirements of a job, and talking to contacts you have. By preparing coping mechanisms and trying out clothes, expressions, camera settings, etc, you can give a polished performance. This all frees up brain space so you can fully immerse yourself into the questions or truly focus on the technical task in front of you.

When all of this clicks into place and you see all your hard work paying off, it's beautiful. All that time you spent learning to code, all that awkward small talk you had that somehow led to deep friendships, all those blog posts you wrote, all that company research you did…it can and will pay off.

You belong in tech. Now, you have all the tools to get there.

Conclusion

'Oh Crap, I Got the Job. Now What?'

Once a contract is signed, it can be hard to believe that your life in tech is really about to begin. You might find imposter syndrome creeping back in or doubt if you're truly ready after all. Luckily, everything you've done up until this point will prepare you for this next step. All of the skills you've learned by reading this book will also prepare you for the professional world of software and application development.

It goes without saying that the programming languages and tools you've learned are the core, transferable skills. However, it's not just about *what* you do, it's about *how* you do it. By applying agile principles to your learning, you'll have learned a lot about the correct mindset for software development. You understand that iterating, reviewing what goes well and what's falling behind, and planning your time are all crucial to continued technical success.

Furthermore, you'll have exercised significant abilities in learning to understand documentation and solve problems. Unlike some of your potential colleagues, you won't have gotten caught in 'tutorial hell', wherein you do so much coding from video tutorials that you never end up solving problems yourself. Instead, you've applied yourself to become an expert at *recalling* concepts when you need them rather than just passively understanding them and becoming trapped in a recognition-only scenario.

All of this is essential for a developer: as a junior, your main job will be to learn and ask questions. Sure, you'll have tasks to do, but the benefit of being a junior is the freedom to ask all the tiny, silly questions that might be tough to get away with later. You should continue having a learning mindset for your entire career, but this first phase is a time when you can enjoy immense freedom to get things wrong and learn from them.

Luckily, as you've also learned in this book, leaning on others is the best way to get ahead. Asking for help is just one aspect of that; showing an interest in *their* story and *their* goals will start some amazing conversations and help deepen your friendships. In time, you can use your ability to network and form communities and find true friends inside your company: those who will raise you up, stand by you, and drop into a call when you're desperate for help and the sprint ends tomorrow.

Your branding kit won't go to waste, either. Be proud of who you are and what you have to offer. If possible, stay active on social networks and continue reaching out to those outside your company. Keep up to date on what's happening. Trust me, there's always something! When you find people who are interested in similar things or (better yet) who have expertise in something completely different but complementary, take the time to invite them to a (virtual, if necessary,) coffee and keep abreast of the tech industry as a whole. You never know when these conversations can help you in your work or when discussing ideas for a project.

If you blog, check to see if your company also has a blog. A lot of the time, technical folk aren't too keen on writing. You can absolutely bring that as an additional skill and offer it to your manager or lead. If they don't need it, try to find an occasional opportunity to put what you pick up into writing and keep your blog active. Not only does it continue to help you learn (just as before), but it's also a great way to get comments and feedback from the community on how you could improve.

Overall, you'll find that the tech industry is far less about objective facts, solitary work, and computer languages and far more about people. Who you work with, how you work with each other, what users want, how the product owner sees it, where the priorities lie—all these common questions rotate around people. If you've built your communication skills effectively, you'll enter the industry at a massive advantage.

One further advantage is the ability to present yourself effectively. Interviewing skills are presentation skills. Everything you learned in this book to help you get ahead in the job market is fully applicable to preparing presentations or conference talks. As a junior, you might not have many responsibilities involving public talks or product presentations with the client. However, you can offer to hold workshops for other team members on a new tool you're using. Alternatively, the skills you learned in coping with nerves and the practice you did speaking into the camera could all help you speak up in meetings when you have an idea or feel more comfortable asking questions when a technical term you've never heard of comes up in a training session.

For me, the most obvious use of job application and interviewing skills are annual reviews. Here, you should state your case clearly and directly about why you should be promoted and/or given a raise. Just as you did with your applications, you should use the NNQ rule and keep track of everything you achieve at work and everything nice people say about you. Again, you should connect the dots between what your workplace expects and what you've achieved. Ideally, you should show how you've gone beyond what they expected and be that technically or in terms of presentations, team support, leadership, or other contributions to the business and its culture.

Although it's intimidating to face a new career and a new workplace, the skills you've built with the help of this book will enable you to meet and exceed those expectations. By continuing to develop your technical abilities, pairing those abilities with your network and content creation skills, and learning how to talk about those achievements openly and with confidence, you can face this new stage of your life with your head held high.

Welcome to tech.

About the Author

Anna McDougall is Director, Product and Engineering (Projects and Organisation) at Axel Springer National Media and Tech GmbH in Berlin. She lives in Leipzig with her husband Alex and her daughter Mathilda, and in her spare time enjoys hiking, making her own popcorn, and dominating the board game Settlers of Catan: Cities and Knights.

You can follow her on:

- Twitter: twitter.com/annajmcdougall
- LinkedIn: linkedin.com/in/annajmcdougall
- YouTube: youtube.com/c/annamcdougall
- Instagram: instagram.com/annajmcdougall

Acknowledgements

Thank you to everyone who helped bring this book into existence, especially to my incredible husband Alex, my little champion Mathilda, and my editor Courtney Meunier.

To my parents, thank you for raising me with so much love, and for writing so many books between you that writing my own didn't seem quite so scary. To my mother, Virginia Nightingale, thank you for being my role model: intelligent, driven, logical, and yet so very kind. You taught me to follow my heart, feed my head, and not shy away from my achievements. To my father, Garry McDougall, thank you for inspiring me with your endless creativity, and for all your support in helping me grow my skills in mathematics, philosophy, debate, and of course computing. I'll never forget our algebra sessions! A special thanks for letting me use your work computer to learn HTML – look where it took me!

A special thanks also to my Kickstarter supporters Philipp Dunkel, Robert Hannah, Steven Boutcher, Thordis Jensen, Shashi Lo, Paola Cantaboni, Zuzanna Kwiatkowska, Stephan Kämper, Elizangela Giffey, Andreas Orth, Vincent Orth, Ondrej Miller, Georgios Krall, Christian Wolff, Rhys Jones, Curtis Swike, Marc Backes, Nicolas Leveque, and Paoli Izquierdo.

Without you all, this book wouldn't be half of what it is.

Printed in Great Britain
by Amazon